THE WISDOM TEACHINGS OF
HARISH JOHARI
ON THE MAHABHARATA

Kurukshetra *by Prabhat Bal.*
Krishna shows Arjuna his glorious shape.

THE WISDOM TEACHINGS OF
HARISH JOHARI
ON THE MAHABHARATA

COMPILED AND EDITED BY

WIL GERAETS

Destiny Books
Rochester, Vermont • Toronto, Canada

Destiny Books
One Park Street
Rochester, Vermont 05767
www.DestinyBooks.com

Destiny Books is a division of Inner Traditions International

Text stock is SFI certified

Library of Congress Cataloging-in-Publication Data

The wisdom teachings of Harish Johari on the Mahabharata / compiled and
edited by Wil Geraets.
     p. cm.
  Includes index.
  ISBN 978-1-59477-379-2 (pbk.)
  1. Mahabharata—Criticism, interpretation, etc. 2. Johari, Harish,
1934–1999—Teachings. I. Geraets, Wil.
  BL1138.26.W57 2011
  294.5'923046—dc22

                                                                    2011006260

Printed and bound in the United States by Lake Book Manufacturing
The text stock is SFI certified. The Sustainable Forestry Initiative® program
promotes sustainable forest management.

10 9 8 7 6 5 4 3 2 1

Text design and layout by Priscilla Baker
This book was typeset in Garamond Premier Pro with Runa Serif used as a display
typeface

Dedicated to Harish Johari who devoted his life to the exploration of human consciousness according to the Tantric and Vedic sciences of India.

Able to grasp the essence of the ancient spiritual wisdom and explain it in contemporary concepts, Harish was a gifted author and lecturer on Indian philosophy including yoga science, chakras, tantra, ayurveda, numerology, and gemology. He was full of inspiration, humor, and laughter, a great cook, painter, sculptor, musician, and storyteller. He left behind a wealth of books, music, paintings, and recorded talks.*

May his words guide us to a clearer understanding of god's creation and human consciousness.

---

*See pages 242–44 and www.sanatansociety.com and www.sanatansociety.org

Contents

ॐ

PART THREE

The Bhagavad Gita

ॐ

PART FOUR

War and Its Aftermath

ॐ

Preface

I first established contact with Harish Johari in 1978 in the Netherlands, where I had grown up in a landscape of villages, agriculture, rivers, and forest. As a teenager, I had become interested in philosophy, and the Beatles' trip to India around that time confirmed the idea that India had much to offer. So I was pleased to find in Harish Johari a teacher capable of conveying that wisdom in contemporary language. During the eighties and the nineties it was an annual feast to spend time with him during his yearly visits to Europe.

The atmosphere in the workshops Harish Johari gave was relaxed and cordial. Most people called him Dada, which means "elder brother" in Hindi. Although the people surrounding him were often discussing various subjects, he loved it when they talked less and painted yantras or the illustrations in the *Chakras* coloring book.* Cooking meals and dining together was an important part of every workshop day. Many times he would say, "No hurry," and on a hot summer's day his lecture might start only at 5:00 p.m.

On the other hand, he criticized students severely for not getting up

---

*Harish Johari's book, *Chakras, Energy Centers of Transformation* (Rochester, Vt.: Destiny Books, 2000), includes black and white illustrations of the chakras, especially designed for coloring.

before sunrise. Especially in the early years he emphasized this point with force. He was a teacher who lived according to his teachings. He stayed awake until late and still got up early. Many of us felt uneasy about getting up early, and we searched for the best excuses. Later Dada became milder in his expression, but he always considered getting up early essential for spiritual life. I tried so hard to get up early. In summertime when the nights were short I would go to bed early, and I'd miss out on lots of city social life. Then in the early mornings I would become very tense as I made all preparations for sitting clean and quietly at sunrise. I decided that it could not be the proper way and stopped trying so hard.

During the nineties, Dada gave a series of workshops devoted to the wisdom of the Mahabharata. I realized that, just as Sanskrit and most European languages share ancient Indo-European roots, the stories of the Mahabharata are ancient roots of Western culture as well. In his lectures on *dharma* (spiritual law, inherent nature, purpose, or duty) Dada explained that every living being and even every object has a purpose to fulfill. During one of the breaks I asked him about the purpose of my life. Since by then he had known me for about twenty years, I expected to get an answer that was tailored according to my personality and situation. He replied, "It is your dharma to live a healthy, happy, and inspired life." That answer was more general than I had expected, but I continue to find it useful, and I feel it can be useful to many who search for meaning in life.

Dada's demise in 1999 was the onset of five black years during which I could sleep only a few hours each night, followed by sheer despair. In those years I started transcribing the tapes of Dada's lectures. I was unhealthy, unhappy, and uninspired, but listening to Dada's voice and typing out his words helped me to accept the loss and find a new way of living. With the help of my friend Peter Marchand, I slowly recovered. Sleeping improved, but mostly after five hours I woke up and it still happens that way. Now getting up before sunrise has become easy! In the early morning hours my mind is fresh and sharp. I found Dada's lectures on Mahabharata a nice subject to employ my mind in the peaceful early hours. I enjoyed the process of organizing Dada's stories and comments from the different workshops and making them more accessible by rephrasing his words, dividing the stories into paragraphs, and putting them into linear timelines.

Part one provides the context for the story of the Mahabharata. The first chapter describes the concept of dharma and its relevance to the story and to our lives. In addition to being duty and purpose, dharma can also be understood as justice, and in Mahabharata justice fights injustice. Chapter 2 explains that the history of humankind is divided into four ages. In the first age almost everybody follows dharma. In the following ages civilization slowly decays, and in the final age hardly anybody follows dharma. Chapter 3 presents the first mythical story situated in the third age, which describes the life of the demon who later will be born as Karna, one of the major characters in the Mahabharata. The stories in chapter 4 offer delightful examples of teaching about truth with fantasy. Chapter 5 presents incidents in the prior lives of Bhishma and Ganga, which are the roots of significant events in the central story.

In part two the story of the Mahabharata begins in earnest. The first two chapters (6 and 7) follow the timeline of Bhishma, the most important character in Mahabharata, describing why he has to be born, how he is born, and how he receives his name. Chapter 8 describes the tangled dynasty into which the founders of the Pandava and Kaurava branches of Bhishma's family are born through immaculate conception. The story of Karna's birth and abandonment by his mother, Kunti, is told in chapter 9. His brothers and cousins are born in chapter 10. Chapters 11 through 14 show the maturation of the children and the expansion of the kingdom but also the growth of trickery and thirst for revenge. The Pandavas are tricked to go into exile. Chapters 14 through 16 are interludes that take place during the exile. Chapter 15 beautifully presents the human psychodrama as the eternal fight between the demons drawing our energy down and the gods trying to direct it upward. In chapter 17 preparations for war are made in earnest.

In part three, composed of chapters 18, 19, and 20, Dada clarifies the Bhagavad Gita, which contains the essence of Indian philosophy, in modern terms. As shown in the frontispiece, Krishna teaches Arjuna about individual and cosmic consciousness, culminating in a vision of everything emanating from the cosmic source and returning to it.

Chapters 21 through 25 in part four deal with the tragedies during and after the great war between the Pandavas and the Kauravas. Chapter 26 goes beyond the actual Mahabharata and tells about the ending of the third era and the beginning of Kali Yuga.

The epilogue explains each main character as a basic aspect of human consciousness. This gives surprising new depth to the previous chapters, as well as making it clear that the Mahabharata is eternally relevant to the game of life.

While the stories of the Mahabharata are entertaining by themselves, it is Dada's comments and explanations that give this text its particular value. He makes it clear that the characters and stories represent human life in general. For example, he explains that Arjuna and Krishna respectively represent individual and cosmic consciousness, Duryodhana represents ego, and Karna jealousy. Other figures in the limelight are Bhishma (sacrifice), Vidura (intellect), Drona (tolerance), Kunti (primordial nature), and Draupadi (energy). Harish Johari is not the first to reveal the deeper layers of the Mahabharata, but his explanations are surprisingly modern and can be understood by people of many cultures.

Many concepts of the ancient Hindu religion are so profound that a lot of time is needed to understand them properly, maybe even more than a lifetime. On the other hand, Dada stated several times that in fact there are really no teachers and no students, since each of us has a spark of god inside; we are just travelers passing some time together. I am happy to have traveled with Dada, who helped me to catch glimpses of the light within, and I welcome you to do the same through the pages of this book.

WIL GERAETS

Acknowledgments

I am grateful to Rob Obermeyer, Pieter Weltevrede, Nan Koehler, and Marian Duys for providing me with tapes from Dada Harish Johari's workshops on the Mahabharata given in the nineties in Utrecht, the Netherlands; Sebastopol, California; and De Pinte, Belgium. I especially wish to thank Peter Marchand for his encouragement to publish this book, for correcting two preliminary versions, and for sending me the beautiful frontispiece by Prabhat Bal. I also give special thanks to Heidi Rauhut, who helped to correct issues concerning English grammar as well as Indian philosophy. Working together on the text was very rewarding. Thanks also to Inner Traditions/Destiny Books and especially to Nancy Yeilding for making Harish Johari's lectures available to a wide public.

Introduction

Maha means "great" and *bharata* means "India," so Mahabharata is the story of the nation of "Great India." It is an epic written in verses and, based on the number of verses, is probably the biggest epic ever written. The full version of Mahabharata has sixty-four volumes, but it has been shortened to make it easier to read. Some versions consist of eighteen or twelve volumes.

Abridged versions in single volumes are also available; in them the story of the war remains, but most of the other stories have been left out. One of these, which is widely available, is *Mahabharata* by C. Rajagopalachari. He became the first governor general of India after Lord Mountbatten left India in 1947. When India became a republic, with Rajendra Prasad as the first president, Nehru as the first prime minister, and Patel as the first home minister, there was no longer any need for a governor general and the post was abolished. By then C. Rajagopalachari was quite an old man, only five feet two inches in size, who wore dark glasses, probably because he had one defective eye. He looked strange, but he was a learned scholar who adapted the Mahabharata and the other major epic of India, the Ramayana, which were then published by the Indian government. Another well-known version is by a swami of the Ramakrishna order. It has a spiritual touch because it comes from a spiritual community, while C. Rajagopalachari's book has a somewhat political touch because it comes from a politician. I mention these two books to show you that there is more than one side to the Mahabharata. In fact, there are as many sides to it as there are interpreters. Everybody sees the story from his own point of view.

The age of the Mahabharata is difficult to ascertain scientifically. The text itself contains a reference to the astronomical constellation under which the great Mahabharata war was fought and that constellation was visible in the sky 6,000 years ago. In those days people were not history conscious in the modern way. Because things wear out quickly in the heat and the rain of India, little physical evidence is left. People who study languages say that Mahabharata was written 3,500 to 4,000 years ago. But the scholars study copies of the scriptures that are less old than the originals. Texts written on palm leaves or on bark last for 3,500 years maximum. Generation after generation the scriptures have been copied over and over and in the process some things could have been changed. For example when I tell about a person informing somebody what was happening, I might say, "He phoned him," because that is the way people are informed nowadays. Still, we can safely say it is 3,500 to 6,000 years old. Compared to the 10,000-year-old stories you can find in the Greek and Persian cultures Mahabharata is not old. Compared with the age of the world or the age of *Homo sapiens* it is new.

The composition of the Mahabharata followed that of the ancient writings of India known as the Vedas, some verses of which might be even 10,000 years old. At first the Vedas existed as independent hymns based on experiences of *rishis* (poet-seers) during their *samadhi* (absorption in supreme consciousness). They were passed on through an oral tradition.

The saint and scholar Vyasa wanted to preserve the hymns for future generations. He knew that Kali Yuga (the "Dark Age") was coming and libraries would be needed, so he wanted to compile and preserve all the existing knowledge (*veda* is *vidya* is "knowledge"). He asked his disciples to visit different sages and collect all the hymns connected with the different branches of knowledge. When the hymns had been collected, Vyasa put them together in four volumes.

Rig Veda, the first Veda, consists of verses with meter. It tells about the world and all substances in the world. It describes plants and minerals, how they are created, their purpose, and how we can work with them. It also deals with astrology, planets, cosmos, mathematics, categories, the three qualities of nature (*gunas*), and the five elements (*tattvas*). Astrology is included as one of the sciences needed for knowing material existence because all substances are connected with planets. Knowledge of Earth, sun, moon, Mars, Mercury, and Jupiter is necessary to understand banana, guava, apple, grape. We can only understand material things by seeing them as solar or lunar energy, as hot or cold, as beneficial or detrimental to life, as sun or moon. All these things are necessary for life.

The second Veda, *Yajur Veda*, consists of prose verses without meter. It tells how life should be organized, the role rituals play in life, how the rituals should be performed, and how they connect human to divine energy.

Sama Veda, the third Veda, contains mantras for chanting, singing, performing rituals, and praying. It was made so that people would be able to sing beautiful mantras in praise of god or to invoke god. It also contains a notation of how the mantras should be sung. About 95 percent of the mantras originate from the *Rig Veda*.

The fourth Veda or *Atharva Veda* deals with human welfare and social life. It deals with cleanliness, purification, healing, *ayurveda* (traditional Indian medicine), and yoga. According to this Veda, yoga was a part of ayurveda. Much later, people who learned yoga but didn't want to learn ayurveda made it a gymnastic game. They started doing up and down, headstand, bow, or serpent, this mudra or that mudra, and they made it a separate science of body culture, glamour, better movement, nice childbirth, and all kinds of things. But yoga wasn't meant for that.

By creating the four Vedas, Vyasa had done a great job. He had

edited and updated all the existing knowledge and made it more accessible for people, but he was not satisfied. He knew that in Kali Yuga
people would get used to dictionaries and encyclopedias, and that they
would think that knowledge lives in books. He knew that people would
become unsure and become slaves of other people's opinions. He knew
that the amount of knowledge available would become overwhelming.
For example, if you are searching for a banana and you enter a small
fruit shop, you can easily select a nice banana. But if I take you to a
huge shop with thousands of bananas and many other things, you will
get confused and you won't know what to take. Similarly Kali Yuga
presents you with billions of books on each subject. Now it has become
a problem how to know which one to trust and read. Vyasa knew this
kind of nonsense would come and that his books on philosophy would
have little meaning because very few people would read philosophy.

When cultures grow up to a particular limit there comes a saturation point, and if there is no way to go up, they have to slide down again.
In the time of the Mahabharata, people had achieved great powers by
doing *sadhana* (spiritual practice), but many of their achievements were
destroyed during and after the war that actually happened during Vyasa's
life. It lasted for eighteen days, and it was like a world war because all
countries sent representatives to participate in it. Vyasa realized that all
the great people and their stories would be forgotten and nobody would
remember how far human civilization had reached. He decided to put
the stories together in the Mahabharata, which is sometimes called the
fifth Veda, to tell future generations about life and to show them how
unimportant things can become important and create problems.

At the beginning of Mahabharata there is small story of how it was
written. Vyasa had a huge amount of stories in his mind. In those days
he could not put them on the hard disc of a computer. He prayed to god
for help and god told him that the elephant-headed god Ganesha was
famous for writing fast and that he was free at the moment. So Vyasa
invoked Ganesha, who appeared and asked him what he wanted. He
said, "In Kali Yuga people will have problems in understanding philoso-

phy. Therefore I want to tell stories that are examples of philosophy. If people can see themselves in the stories that will help them to understand." Ganesha agreed to write everything down. He did not have a well-manufactured pen that would last for writing such a big epic. So he broke off one of his tusks, which had a fine point, and with that he wrote the whole story. Traditional books of the Mahabharata often show a picture at the beginning depicting Vyasa sitting on one side and Ganesha sitting on the other side with lots of paper.

Although Vyasa was a saint, he had a little ego, thinking he knew so much that it would be difficult to write down. For the sake of good health, Ganesha wanted to lower Vyasa's ego, so he demanded that Vyasa dictate without pause or else he would leave. Vyasa did not want to lose Ganesha, so he had to keep him busy writing. When the story would get less interesting, he dictated things that were not really necessary for the story such as explanations of a character or philosophical statements. That way the Mahabharata epic became longer and more beautiful.

People sometimes say that Mahabharata is an epic created by a poet and that it is full of exaggeration and imagination but without truth. According to the story, one of the major characters, Krishna, was born in Mathura, brought up in Vrindavan, and educated in the Himalayas. All the land had been claimed by various kings, so he went to the ocean and asked for some land. The ocean receded and a small area came out where he made his own kingdom, which was called Dvaraka. Then, after Krishna left the world, the ocean occupied most parts of Dvaraka. Quite recently, the old town of Dvaraka was discovered under water and excavations are still going on. Some of the findings from those excavations show that there is some historical truth behind the story. When a poet creates a story he has the poetic license to use his imagination and exaggerate elements of the story and also to add new elements. So Mahabharata is not a historical account because Vyasa mixed historical truth with imagination as many writers do. But it contains various characters with whom we can easily identify, and when we recognize similar situations in our life, it helps us to deal with them.

It is a quality of Vyasa to create things that are normally not possible and such supernatural elements make the story more interesting. Similarly, *Alice in Wonderland* is so popular because it brings you into a fantasy world. Mahabharata has supernatural beings like celestial dancers, nymphs, *gandharvas* (celestial musicians), demons, and mixtures of gods, humans, and demons. It includes the stories of all the incarnations of the god Vishnu, including Rama and Krishna, and the lion, boar, and fish. The stories in Mahabharata may be true or they may be just imagination. In any case you should listen to them with your right hemisphere like a child, because then you can allow a monkey to fly and a bird to talk in a human voice about the future. Such stories educate us in a right-hemisphere way about human life, behavior, and consciousness.

Most of the stories that are connected with culture and tradition are automatically heard by the right hemisphere of the brain of people from that culture. To me the Mahabharata stories seem true because I have been hearing them for thousands of years and they have become a part of my genetic information; that produces faith and I cannot disbelieve them even if I wanted to. For the same reason you cannot believe them even though you would like to. Lack of that particular gene inside you creates doubt, and you will hear them as just stories. You will never believe them although you would like to understand the inner meaning on the intellectual level. If I say an elephant was flying, you will say that elephants don't fly. But if I tell you a story of a flying elephant, you can accept it. Stories don't alarm the defense mechanism of the mind. When you can listen to it as a tale without questioning it, the great teaching behind the story finds its place inside you.

PART ONE

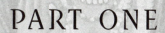

Setting the Scene

1

Dharma in the Mahabharata and in Life

Dharma plays an important role in Mahabharata, so it is important to understand its full meaning. Many people confuse dharma with religion and rules of good conduct like, "Thou shall not steal" or "Treat thy neighbor as thyself." Such rules are necessary and helpful, but dharma is more than ethics. Your dharma is the real purpose of your life. Your dharma is your duty. In the Bhagavad Gita, Krishna speaks about *svadharma* (personal duty).

Dharma Is Purpose of Life

Everybody has to follow his or her own dharma. The dharma of a teacher is to teach and the dharma of a student is to go into the deeper meanings of the teachings. The dharma of a mother is to take care of her children and the dharma of a father is to ensure the security and safety of his wife and children. The dharma of a tape recorder is to record sound if the play and the record buttons are pressed and to play sound when only the play button is pressed. When it stops working it is repaired or discarded. As long as this cup holds liquids it is following its dharma and it has meaning, but as soon as it leaks it does not fulfill its dharma anymore and it is thrown away.

The dharma of fire is to burn and the dharma of water is to extinguish fire. Suppose there is a fire going on and I throw water on it but the water does not follow its dharma and just for one day it acts like gasoline. Then I will say that the water is not doing its job. Similarly, if a person does not follow his dharma, he loses the meaning of life and we say he is not behaving responsibly. If a mother doesn't take care of her children, we say she is not a good mother.

Dharma is different for every individual and each person has to decide what his or her own dharma is. You are the final judge of what your dharma is and what action is in accordance with your inherent nature. But following your inherent nature does not mean that you follow every feeling from within. Lots of people say they do what they feel but they are not really following their inherent nature because what they feel is created by genetic code, environment, education, and culture.

It is difficult to see your dharma by introspection. Because of our artificial way of living we lack proper understanding of our personality. Living a more natural life would make it easier to see our dharma. In addition, our view is obscured by temporary benefits and selfish motives. Therefore people consult saints and realized beings with universal wisdom to ask about their dharma. Then their questions are answered according to their physical, psychological, and environmental makeup.

When you are judging an action yourself, you have to ask yourself if the action is good for you, good for the people around you, good for humanity in general, and good for planet Earth. If it is, then go ahead; otherwise refrain from the action.

Dharma Is Truth

Some Sanskrit couplets that I learned as a child describe the principles of dharma in a simple way. Singing them made me feel good and still

I sing them occasionally. One of my favorites is: *Satyam bruyat pri-yam bruyat na bruyat satyam apriyam priyam cha nanrtam bruyat esha dharma sanathanah.* It means: "Speak truth and speak it pleasantly. Don't speak untruth and don't speak truth in an unpleasant way. Don't talk about things that are pleasing but untrue or things that are true but private."

Truth can be told many ways and the modern way is to speak it bluntly, which was considered uncivilized once upon a time. Truth that does not lead to good things and good feelings should not be told. Most people avoid talking about personal things that barely concern anybody else like the intimate relationship with their partner, but some people like to talk about such things.

Everybody has the right and the duty to be honest. Everybody should be able to call a spade a spade and not talk diplomatically say-ing, "It looks like a spade, but at the moment I cannot say it is a spade because it could be something else." Many people tell lies just to please others. When they say, "Oh you are very good," "Oh I am so happy to see you!" or "It was so great to meet you!" it is only to please you. It may be nice to hear but if it is not truth don't say it. Hostesses in an airplane may smile and appear happy but I know they are angry. That also should not be done; you should allow yourself to express your feelings but on the other hand you should not scare others. Sometimes in a relationship between and man and a woman one scares the other by remaining silent, giving a heavy look, and creating a heavy atmo-sphere; after some time the other feels obliged to leave. Lots of couples who come for consultation are caught in that kind of trip. That is also not dharma.

Many people thrive on the fear of others, such as doctors, thera-pists, or priests who scare you with hell. They don't mind telling you the truth even if it disturbs you. However, sometimes following dharma means not telling clearly what the other wants to know. When a person asks me about the attributes that numerology associates with their par-ticular number then I will only tell as much as is not disturbing. When you visit an astrologer who does not know you, he will not be interested in you and tell you everything. But when he has started knowing you, he will only tell you as much as will not disturb you.

Dharma is being true, not telling anything untrue, not exaggerating truth, nor undermining or manipulating truth, but presenting truth in a pleasant form. A lie is *adharma* (a violation of dharma) and should not be spoken. Even speaking a lie out of consideration for somebody and not wanting to disturb the person is adharma and it creates bad karma* even if it is spoken to save somebody's life. But poets, storytellers, and writers have a license to tell lies. They may say, "The man was as brave as a lion" or "Bhima had the power of one thousand elephants," but it is a lie. (Horsepower would have been okay but not elephant-power.) That kind of exaggeration is called poetic license and is found in all scriptures and epics. Also in life it can get difficult to follow the truth strictly. The story of the honest man and the cow illustrates that dharma can be ambiguous.

◦❧◦

The Honest Man and the Cow

There was an assembly of saints who used to ask questions, and one man used to play the wise guy and answer the questions. When he was asked under which circumstances it is okay to tell a lie, he told the following story.

There was a man who was reputed to be honest. All his life he lived in a hut near the village practicing dharma. Most of the time he was meditating or helping others. He never spoke a lie and never did anything wrong. One day he saw a cow running. She passed his hut and disappeared into the jungle. After a few minutes some people came with swords in their hands. They were searching for the cow and wanted to slaughter it. They knew the honest man never spoke a lie and asked him if he had seen a cow passing by. He said he had, but when they asked him which direction it had gone, he pointed in two

---

*Karma literally means "action," but it is often used, as in this case, to also refer to the consequences of an action, which can come to the person later, even in later lifetimes.

opposite directions. The butchers could not understand him and they left.

A little later one of them came back and asked why he had not clearly pointed out the way the cow had gone. He said, "I wanted to tell the truth, but I also wanted to save the cow. If I had pointed clearly the way she had gone, you would have killed her. One hand was pointing to the way she went and the other hand was just balancing and that confused you. With my gestures and my talking I wasted half an hour and I gave the cow time to escape, but I did not tell a lie."

The man asked, "I would really like to know what your dharma was this time."

The honest man said, "It was really my dharma to tell a lie. I should have told you a lie by pointing in the wrong direction, but I could not do that. So I pointed in the right direction, but I confused you with my other hand. So I did not point it out clearly, but in a way I did not tell a lie."

Then the man asked, "What do you think you did?"

The honest man said, "I know I created bad karma because either I should not have told you anything or I should have told you the truth. Observing silence would have been the best, but you all came with swords and you were in a mood to kill, so I was afraid to lose my life if I kept silent. By not telling you exactly which direction the cow went I wanted to save her life as well as mine. That way I think I did my dharma."

Dharma and Tradition

Following the tradition of the family, town, country, or culture to which you belong is called *kula char* (family tradition) or *loka char* (general tradition). If you grow up in an environment where everybody follows a traditional role then doing the same is not adharma. For example, hamburger eating is not adharma when it is done in a culture where it is a common practice to prepare and eat something like that. But from the point of view of the body that has to digest the hamburger, it is full of toxins; in that way it is adharma to produce such products. Glorifying it and creating a ritual for it would certainly be adharma.

However, some tribes do ritual human sacrifice for a god or goddess. For them it is a holy worship to kill a man, whereas morally and ethically it is a crime. They will not feel it as a crime because it is the tradition of their tribe. The practice itself is much against dharma, but when it is tradition in that society, the followers are not doing any adharma and will not be responsible for any bad karma following their action.

To some extent it is your dharma to follow the customs of the land where you were born. But when you evolve then you don't see yourself only as a member of your tribe, country, or culture but also as a part of the cosmic play. Then your dharma changes and you have to see if an action will cause harm or not. If it causes pain and suffering, then it is not to be done. Some people don't follow dharma because they have no good examples. Education and right judgment needs example, and if nobody around you is following dharma you will never know what dharma is. For example, in a certain town, it may be that nobody in the whole town wakes up early except the people who are ill or working on night shifts.

Although there are disadvantages with the caste system, it is well accepted that it produces better craftsmen, better artists, and people who are better able to deal with a particular problem of society. Through genetic information the caste system creates better skills. For example, a son of a jeweler becomes a better jeweler because in his genes the knowledge of working with metals, gems, and jewelry is already there. Allowing everybody to become whatever they want is too general and is not a healthy way of growing. For example, if I work as a teacher and my son as something else and his son as something else then we all may be capable of doing our jobs, but we will lack the advantage and confirmation of our genes.

Practicing the same thing generation after generation has advantages. In Bareilly, Shanti and her husband wash our laundry. For hundreds of generations her family has been only washing laundry. One of their three sons is living in Delhi and doing business, but the other two live in Bareilly and help their parents. When the tradition of doing this work started there were no commercial markets to supply cleaning aids, so the family had to try and work out formulas to remove stains. Now Shanti does not have to buy detergents and spot removers from the market. If I stand in the river and wash the clothes like she does then in two days my hands will get sore, and I will not be able to do anything. But they have been doing it for generations and they can do it eight hours a day without getting tired.

In our country a son of a cobbler is a cobbler, a son of a washerman is a washerman, a son of a blacksmith is a blacksmith, and a son of a carpenter is a carpenter. If you are born in a brahmin family and you start fighting like a warrior you are not following your own dharma. If you were born in a warrior family and you open a shop and sell garments like some priests (brahmins) do then you are following the dharma of a merchant. Nowadays this system is changing because with proper education anybody can become an officer or a carpenter.

Constitution and Circumstances Are Guides to Dharma

The body is the most important determinant of dharma. First you should follow the dharma of your body, then the dharma connected with your mind, and then the dharma connected with your spirit. But most people ignore the dharma of their body and go with the dharma of their mind. They forget about dharma of the spirit and that dharma is mostly unknown.

The first factor determining your dharma is your constitution. If you have to choose a profession, then see what your body and mind combined can do best. If your inside supports you in explaining the meanings of scriptures then your dharma is to study scriptures and find out their inner meanings. It can be your dharma to find out the faults in everything. Many people search for faults in equipment that is not working. They find the faults and write them down and then they call specialists to come and repair the equipment. Once you have a profession it is your dharma to do your job the best you can. To do your job efficiently and precisely, you need knowledge and a method to handle your job in a right way.

Your body depends on which part of the planet you were born, the altitude, and the geographical environment in which you live. The dharma of an Eskimo differs from the dharma of a tropical person. The body is connected with planet Earth but also with sun, moon, Mars, Mercury, Venus, Jupiter, and Saturn. So body dharma is quite big.

Because our body is connected with Earth it is connected with life and it is our dharma to consciously work with all life that exists. We should not unnecessarily destroy life nor unnecessarily help life but help it as much as we can. It is our dharma to be vegetarians because violence and eating meat create problems. When you eat meat the bad chemicals in your body make you feel like you have used violence and the word *violence* becomes big in your head. I have seen Western people paying importance to violence because they like rare steak from which blood comes out from both sides of the mouth.

At the same time, we can never avoid violence completely. We constantly kill bacteria by breathing them in and also when walking. Words like *violence, aggression,* and *fight* have real meaning when they are done for selfish motives. If you eat a chicken when fruits and other nice foods are available then you are doing it only for the taste and you are doing something bad. But when you are starving and there is no other food available, then it is your dharma to save your life by killing the chicken and eating it. You can eat it to save your life but not for luxury. Potatoes are alive; if you put them in the ground they will develop roots and start growing. You could think that it is bad to peel potatoes alive, put them in a metal pot, boil them, and eat them. But dharma is not only philosophically analyzing everything but also understanding the dharma of the moment: if I am hungry I need potatoes.

That is the second factor determining dharma—the situation in which you are at a given moment. At one moment the dharma of the farmer is to take care of the seeds. When he has put the seeds into the ground it is his dharma to give proper manure and proper water to the ground. When the plant grows it is his dharma to protect the plant. When the fruits come it is his dharma to protect them. And when the fruits are ripe it is his dharma to pluck them and give them to somebody who can use them before they rot.

The hero of the Ramayana, Rama, says, "There is no higher dharma than helping others, thinking about the welfare of others, and service to humanity." Nonviolence is considered high dharma and harming or disturbing people is definitely considered adharma. Harming others and creating problems for others is guided by selfishness. When we are no longer selfish we can follow dharma. If you want to support dharma and not favor adharma, you should also see how to help justice in a particular situation and oppose what is not right. The highest dharma is to endure losses and just help. This is illustrated by the traditional Indian story of the saint and the scorpion.

⊙⅄⊚

The Saint and the Scorpion

A saint was taking a bath in a river. His disciple was sitting on the bank of the river watching the saint and taking care of his belongings, which were little more than a mala *(prayer beads) and a bowl for drinking water and begging. A scorpion came floating by, struggling for survival. The saint put his hand under it so that it could sit and be safe. He started moving toward the riverbank to release it. After a minute the scorpion had dried up a little from the warmth of the hand and it felt alive again. It lifted its tail and stung the hand of the saint. Although it was painful, the saint did not throw the animal off. He kept it in his hand and continued walking. Even when the scorpion stung again the saint did not throw it off. He waited until he reached the bank and put the scorpion safely on the ground.*

His disciple asked, "Why did you let the scorpion sting you twice?"

The saint said, "It is his dharma to sting and it is my dharma to save life.

When the scorpion does not leave his dharma of stinging how can I leave my dharma of saving him?"

———◆———

Dharma belongs to the very nature of beings. But human beings have consciousness. Our decisions about dharma are based on the role we are playing, on what we think we are, and how we live. If it had been a scientist who needed to collect species of scorpions, he would have immediately frozen it and put it in a glass bottle with a label "Found in 1987 on the bank of river Ganga." We each have a different way of deciding what our dharma is. I will not say the scientist is wrong to put the scorpion in a bottle so people can study it. By the way, did you know that the scorpion carries her eggs right on her back? When they are full grown, the baby scorpions come out and eat the body of the mother. The mother follows her dharma and lets them eat her body. She survives as long as she can; then, when many of her kind have come out, she has to go.

Following the Dharma of the Sun and Moon

The sun is connected with you as it is connected with Earth. It is responsible for all life on the planet and for the warmth inside you, which responds to the environment. Without that warmth you would be a cold person. The sun is connected with your intellect.

Following the dharma of the sun includes respecting people who are your elders, people with knowledge, and people in positions of authority. You have to follow the dharma connected with the sun. We all have the dharma of getting up and cleaning ourselves before sunrise so that we can be ready to enjoy the environment that becomes pleasant at sunrise. The first rays of sun bring ultraviolet light that charges the atmosphere with negative ions and causes a light breeze full of oxygen and vital energy (*prana,* life-force). Following dharma connected with the sun includes making use of that energy. But not everybody follows this dharma.

There is also dharma connected with the moon. A new moon creates a particular body chemistry and an emotional low tide, whereas a full moon causes an emotional high tide. This is because of the gravitational pull of the moon on water and 80 percent of the human body is water. The high and low tides inside you are connected with the moon inside you. The moon inside you corresponds with the cooling liquids inside your body that keep you calm and cool, everything alkaline in your body, everything feminine in your body, and everything that nourishes you and makes you grow and develop.

2

The Four Ages of Time

In the Western way of thinking about evolution, humans first walked on four feet and lived in caves like animals. Later humans walked on two feet and had long arms. Finally *Homo sapiens* came with shorter arms and a bigger brain. But Hindu scriptures sketch a different picture. According to Indian tradition time is divided into four ages or *yugas:* Satya Yuga, Treta Yuga, Dvapara Yuga, and Kali Yuga. The duration of the yugas is proportional: 4:3:2:1 (or 8:4:2:1). With Kali Yuga lasting 432,000 solar years, it can be calculated that the four yugas together last 4.3 million solar years (or 6.5 million solar years); some sources even mention a duration of 8 billion solar years.

A Day of Brahma

The four yugas together equal one day of Brahma. At the end of the day of Brahma, Kali Yuga ends in total destruction. Then there is a period of rest for as long as there was action; this is the night of Brahma. So one *kalpa*, which is one day plus one night of Brahma, lasts 8.6 million solar years (or more). After the night of Brahma, creation starts again. Many times life has been created and destroyed and this game never stops.

Satya Yuga, the golden period or the age of truth (*satya*), was closest to the origin of humankind. Then the whole earth was Mother Earth and there was no struggle for life. Because nature provided an abundance of flowers, fruits, and foods, there was no office, no industry, and no work. Because life was simpler and there were fewer distractions, people were closer to truth. They spent their time in an ideal way in the pursuit of truth, living in truth and by truth, following the law of dharma. Everybody was honest and all people were brothers and sisters. There was enough time to think about laws of conduct, write scriptures, and do good things. Many scriptures explaining truth come from this time.

The second age, Treta Yuga, was the time of Rama (as depicted in the Ramayana). People were still honest, but Earth did not provide enough food, so they had to start agriculture and make their own clothes to survive. Among a million people only one became a demon and everybody else prayed to god to reestablish peace.

In the third age, Dvapara Yuga, the number of people and businesses increased. There were more territories and more boundaries. Small kingdoms started. Moral principles and social laws lost their value; in such a changing context, everything had to change. Mahabharata was written at the end of Dvapara Yuga and it contains stories of Satya, Treta, and Dvapara Yuga. It tells how truth became powerless and how lies and bad things prevailed. But even when truth loses power it is not broken and it will mobilize divine powers to fight the materialistic forces of this world.

The age in which we are living is called Kali Yuga, the "Dark Age." It started some 6,000 years ago. It will last for 432,000 years, so it has only just begun. Individualistic feelings increase and small pieces of land like Holland, Belgium, and England have become independent kingdoms with their own character and their own language. The depth of true knowledge is lost and only superficial knowledge of matter and mind (psychology) remains. In the Dark Age people are unsure about the future and it is typical for this age that people expect this world to end soon, but it will continue. To imagine that this wretched and polluted world has to go on for thousands of years is really torturous; please don't think it will happen like that.

Six thousand years ago there were less things for people to think about. Going to a country far away took years. Now our speed of movement has increased so much that I can travel every year from India to Europe to give talks. But our instinct and our way of thinking have not changed. We still have the problems of jealousy, of wanting more territory, more power, more wealth, and more popularity. Humans have been afflicted by these things for millennia.

Civilization's Descent

We like to think that we are more civilized, but actually civilization is going down. The characteristic difference between the yugas is that the good qualities increasingly need more effort. In Satya Yuga and Treta Yuga something done by wrong means could not be right. At the end of Dvapara Yuga people started caring less about how things were accomplished. In Kali Yuga people have become more selfish and they want to get their job done somehow or the other. In Satya Yuga people were honest. It was exceptional that somebody broke a promise or somebody was dishonest. Earth, trees, and fruits belonged to everybody and there were no problems about property because nobody had property. Now in Kali Yuga being honest is as difficult as it was to be dishonest in Satya Yuga.

Look at the condition of the water in the river Ganga (Ganges). Its source is a melting glacier. Even today crystal clear water is coming out of it. In Haridwar* the water is collected as *amrita* (nectar of life). People keep it in bottles for years and it does not spoil. Afterward the sewer lines and the waste products of factories pollute the river and by the time it reaches Calcutta, the water has become injurious for health.

---

*Haridwar, a town in north India, is a famous place of pilgrimage on the banks of the Ganges river.

Similarly cultures start pure and then slowly get polluted by so-called prophets, saints, babas, and gurus, which is all cultural nonsense.

Mahabharata describes the transitional period from Dvapara Yuga to Kali Yuga when almost all values of dharma are lost and humans stray farther away from truth. It is the story of the downfall of human values and ideals. In Kali Yuga only exceptional people like an incarnation of god himself can follow dharma. We can talk about dharma, but we cannot follow it. For example, there was a big conference about ecology and lots of people went there by airplanes to attend it. They were polluting the environment to go and talk about how to be friendly with the environment. Following the simple law of dharma to leave nature in its free way and not to destroy the environment has become difficult, but we cannot go back to the time when we were living with the environment instead of destroying it.

Kali Yuga is a time of challenge. We have to be more alert and exert more effort to be right because wrong things are available everywhere. Because of commerce you can get things from an Indian store by UPS the next day just by a simple phone call. You can go around the world and keep on buying and selling just with a credit card. There is more chance to be spoiled and more chance to be lazy or crazy. Previously women used to do their own laundry and clean their own houses, but now machines are doing it and just folding clothes feels like a lot of work.

Somebody may say you can follow dharma by following the eight-step way of Patanjali's *ashtanga* (eight-limbed) yoga, from *yama* (rules of conduct) and *niyama* (discipline), *asana* (postures), *pranayama* (control of breath), *pratyahara* (bringing senses inward), *dharana* (concentration), *dhyana* (uninterrupted meditation), to *samadhi* (complete equilibrium). But observing the five yamas (truth, nonviolence, no sex, no greed, no attachment to possession) seems impossible; just observing truthfulness seems difficult. And the five niyamas (stay clean, be satisfied, control the mind, look inside, worship god) look strange.

Gandhi tried to follow truth (satya) and nonviolence (*ahimsa*), which are only two of the five yamas. And at the age of fifty-five, after he had fathered many children, he tried to follow *brahmacharya,* sexual continence. Even at that age it is good, but it is not the real concept of brahmacharya. Nowadays people don't abstain from sex even when they are standing with one leg in their grave. The concept of brahmacharya has gone. I know lots of psychologists who promote masturbation and other nonsense, which was supposed to be adharma but now in the name of psychology has become dharma. Psychology is giving a new dharma, which is pseudo dharma. They think it is necessary to prevent you from freaking out. They say things like "You can slap your father because otherwise you will repress your anger and get crazy. If you can't beat him directly just take a pillow and beat it saying, 'I hate you, I kill you,' . . . and pay a hundred dollars."

The Bull of Dharma

Dharma is represented as a bull because a bull continuously follows his dharma. He ploughs the fields, carries loads, produces progeny, and keeps the cows giving milk. He helps humanity for just a little hay. The bull is a humble servant and a good friend of human beings.

In Satya Yuga the bull of dharma is standing on his four feet comfortably. Everybody follows dharma; it is a way of life. If somebody does not follow dharma then people make a great fuss about it: "Oh god this man broke his promise. Get him out of society." Nobody talks to him anymore. By the end of Satya Yuga other factors grow.

In Treta Yuga the bull has to stand on three feet, which is not too hard. Following dharma becomes just a little difficult. People become a little selfish and sometimes they deviate from the path of dharma. It is no problem to break your promise once in while.

In Dvapara Yuga the bull has to stand on two feet, which is easy for human beings and penguins but difficult for a bull. He is standing on one front foot and diagonally one hind foot, so he has problems balancing his body and he cannot live an ordinary life anymore. In Dvapara Yuga people have problems in following dharma. Selfishness increases and breaking your promise once in a while is not enough anymore. You should be allowed to be off the track for a couple of times in your life.

In Kali Yuga the bull has a hard time balancing himself on only one foot, doing gymnastics like a clown in a circus. Following good ideals of life or doing yoga has become extremely difficult.

The period of Mahabharata was a period of crisis like today. Today the crisis is high because there are synthetic problems created by people. Viruses and bacteria for biological warfare are created in labs. These things are much more fatal than at the time of the Mahabharata, but in essence the problem is the same: the bull of dharma is out of balance.

3

Power and Penance

Power is energy, is Shakti, which can only be handled by Shiva. Shakti is all movement while Shiva is inactively sitting in samadhi. Shakti can only be canalized into a higher channel by inactivity. That is why Shiva is the only one who can be the husband of Shakti. Everybody has his own desires and ambitions. Everybody wants to become the king of the universe and reorganize the whole world. So everybody uses Shakti for the fulfillment of desires and ambitions.

When somebody becomes too powerful only a saint or a divine being can control his power, like in the story of Sahasrabahu.

Nara and Narayana Vanquish the Demon

In Treta Yuga there was a rakshasa *(demon) with a thousand arms. His name was Sahasrabahu (sahasra is "thousand," and* bahu *is "arms"). Because he could handle a thousand weapons at the same time and all of his opponents had only two hands, or maybe four or eight, he was practically invincible. He had done a lot of sadhana. He would take a mala in each right hand and do mantra japa (mantra repetition) with 500 malas at one time.* That way he did*

---

*Mantras are "sounds that generate power"; mantra japa is often done with the aid of a mala, each bead on the string being associated with the repetition of the mantra, similar to the use of a rosary for prayer.

as much japa in one hour as a person could do in 500 days. By doing japa and puja (worship) his meditation had gained a lot of power.

One day Sahasrabahu asked Brahma to let him become immortal, but Brahma said, "I cannot give you a boon that you will never die, but you can ask for a boon that you think will make you immortal."

Then the demon asked for a threefold boon. The first part was that only somebody who had done sadhana for a thousand years in a row should be able to fight him. The second part was that a single person should not be able to kill him. Only a team of persons (virtually impossible to put together) could do it. The third part of the boon was that he should always remain free and never become imprisoned.

Brahma agreed and gave him the boon just as he had asked.

The rakshasa thought nobody could do sadhana for a thousand years and then defeat him with his thousand arms. His power made him crazy and he started all kinds of power games. He did lots of bad things like forcing people to worship him instead of their god. He chased Indra (king of the gods and lord of heaven) out of heaven and all the gods had to run away and hide under the ocean. He disturbed the balance of the earth and became the king of the earth.

Anybody in trouble can ask Brahma, Vishnu, or Shiva for help. The gods were getting so desperate that they decided to go to Vishnu and they asked for his help, "We cannot handle this rakshasa. He is too powerful and he is destroying the entire earth. People stopped worshipping us because he became the king and people have to worship him. Now we don't get our share of emotions and we are getting weak. Please help us before we starve."

The gods spoke like this because they eat emotions rather than food. That's why when I do my puja before I eat, I take out a little bit of the food, close my eyes, and chant a mantra. That way I send my emotions to the gods. The food remains here and afterward it is given to the birds.

Vishnu said, "The problem is that this guy is too much and I cannot fight him. After hard penance he has obtained a boon that no one person can kill him. So we need two. If you could bring one more Vishnu from somewhere, then there would be two Vishnus and we could fight. But you cannot bring one more Vishnu."

Then Brahma said, "Come on, you can do it. You can create two parts of you. And with these two parts you can do it."

Vishnu agreed. He divided himself into two brothers who were born on Earth. One was called Nara and the other was called Narayana. Nara *means* "man" *and* Narayana *means* "lord of men."

Immediately after birth the two brothers engaged themselves in sadhana, because the other part of the demon's boon was that the one who could kill him must have done a thousand years of practice. They went to Badrinath in the Himalayas and started doing tapasya (self-discipline). Sahasrabahu had taken abode in that area because hardly anybody could survive there. Badrinath is at an altitude of 11,000 feet where no trees are growing and there are few shadows. When the sun shines the light is strong because of the altitude and the light reflected by the snow-covered areas, so a person burns quickly, making it difficult to do sadhana.

Still, Nara and Narayana became yogis and went through a thousand years of penance at Badrinath before they challenged Sahasrabahu.* After a long time they were able to chop off one arm. By continuously fighting the demon they managed to cut his arms one by one. It took them a long time because the demon had taken a vow that he would never say anything untrue and he would never do anything wrong like gambling or dishonesty. He followed that vow so vehemently that he had no weakness where the gods could attack him.

When Sahasrabahu had only two arms left he realized that there was no escape from the two brothers and that he was going to get killed. In fear for his life he ran to Garuda, the birdlike creature who carries Vishnu. He said, "I am a good man, the only thing is that I displayed my power too much and scared everybody. Please save me."

Garuda said, "I cannot save you, but my elder brother Aruna can. He is the

---

*Now when you visit Badrinath you can see two mountains representing Nara and Narayana.

charioteer of the sun god Surya. Go and ask him." Aruna was lame because he had half legs only. When he had been in the egg his mother had not been able to resist seeing how much he had grown and she broke the egg before the lower part of his body had developed. Surya took him as his charioteer so that he did not have to walk. He was just sitting in his chariot going from east to west and west to east all the time. When Sahasrabahu asked Aruna for his help, he allowed him to hide in the chariot where nobody would find him. Vishnu and the gods were searching but could not find him and he was safe.

When Aruna told Surya he had hidden somebody in the chariot to save his life, the sun god did not know what to do about it. He thought, "I cannot keep on hiding this guy in my chariot all the time." But he knew that in the Mahabharata period two forms of Vishnu would again take birth—Narayana as Krishna and Nara as Arjuna—and that they would then finish off Sahasrabahu incarnated as Karna.

————◆————

4

Wish-fulfilling Trees and Cows

Indians love fantasy and Indian mythology tells stories of wish-fulfilling trees and cows. It is fantasy but it is truth because truth is beyond words and it is better represented by fantasy than by facts. Art, music, poetry, and literature are needed to represent truth. Look for the truths that are told by the following stories.

The Wish-fulfilling Tree at the Gate of Heaven

One day Saint Narada came to a king and they got absorbed in talking about law, truth, and god. A good listener inspires the person who is talking, and the king was so interested that Narada kept on talking. Then he remembered he had an appointment with Indra and said, "Oh it is getting late, I have to go. I must finish here and go to meet Indra. When I have time I'll come back and talk with you again."

The king said, "If I could come with you up to the door of heaven then we could talk a little more. And when you enter heaven we could split up and I could go back home."

29

Narada agreed and so they continued their discussion and went up to the gate of heaven. Narada said, "King, you cannot go further because it is prohibited for men of flesh and bone to enter heaven. Either you stay here or return to your kingdom; I am going inside."

The king asked, "How much time will it take for you to come back?"

Narada said, "Half an hour."

The king said, "I will relax here half an hour until you come back." He did not know that half an hour of divine life is equal to thousands of years of human life. Many kingdoms and dynasties change in half an hour of divine time.

Narada went through the gate and the king sat down under a tree near the gate of heaven. It was a wish-fulfilling tree, so when the king said to himself, "How nice it would be if there were a cool breeze," immediately there came a breeze. Enjoying the breeze, he said to himself, "It would be even nicer if some ladies from my harem would give me a massage." Immediately all the ladies from his harem appeared and started giving him a foot massage. He said, "I thought about it and it happened. But if my wife comes here and sees me like this she will be angry." Immediately his wife came because a wish-fulfilling tree fulfills every wish. So while he was getting a foot massage from all the harem ladies, his wife appeared. She became furious and then the king had to run away from there and go home.

———◆———

The next story takes place in Dvapara Yuga. It is about Saint Vasishta who was the mindborn son of Brahma the creator. He was one of the greatest gurus ever and he taught Rama. He had a wish-fulfilling cow called Kamadhenu (*kama* is "desire," *dhenu* is "cow") and the story shows Kamadhenu's power (so it is about cow power rather than horse power). Kamadhenu has a cow's body, horse's neck, peacock's tail, and swan's feathers. It is inside everybody. However, as long as you live in the world and you have desires, obligations, and responsibilities, this cow is not available to you. But when you live free from worldly desires and selfishness, when you share all you have with everybody, then you can use the cow like saints can.

⟨❖⟩

The King and the Wish-fulfilling Cow

Once King Vishvamitra was on his way home after a victory over his enemies. Before reaching home he visited Saint Vasishta who was living humbly in a jungle hut. When you go to a teacher you are supposed to be without ego, but the king took his army with him. He paid his homage to his teacher and they had tea together. When the king was about to leave, the saint asked him to come back in the evening and have food with him. The king, who had a big ego, treated the saint as somebody ordinary. He said it was not possible because he had just fought a war and he had a big army with him including warriors, horses, and elephants, who all had to eat as well. Surely his teacher could not feed a whole army. The saint said that it was no problem and that the soldiers and animals were invited as well.

In the early evening the king sent his commander in chief to the saint's hut to see what was happening. The commander saw the saint sitting in meditation but nobody was cooking anything. He returned to the king and told him the saint was busy worshipping as if he had forgotten he had invited them for food. The king thought, "When we reach there he will remember he invited us for food and maybe then he will cook."

When the king and his army arrived at the saint's place they got a warm welcome. Everybody remained standing because in the jungle there were no chairs and no carpets. The saint realized he needed seats for the people to sit on. He went to his cow and said, "Mother, my king and his men have come here. Please arrange comfortable seats for them." Along with her out-breath, hundreds of divine beings came out of the cow's nose carrying nice chairs and tables. They offered everybody seats suitable to their designation. The king was impressed because even he could not offer everybody the seat that he deserved.

When they all had sat down the king said, "Sir, we are hungry, so we would like to start supper."

The saint got up, went to his cow, and said, "Mother, my king and his people are hungry. Please provide them with food." Again divine persons came out from the cow and they asked everybody to close their eyes and think about the food they liked the most. When the guests opened their eyes they found in front of them plates full of their favorite food. Most of them had chocolates, hot dogs, hamburgers, and ice cream with coca cola. It was impressive; not even the rich king who had won over three fourths of the earth could have offered so many people plates heaped with the food of their own choice.

After they ate the king said to the saint, "Sir, we enjoyed having food with you. You are living in the jungle so you don't really need much. But I am a king who regularly has guests from different countries that need to be served properly. So I need this cow more than you do. The best things of the kingdom should belong to the king. So please give your cow to me."

The saint said, "My son, this cow cannot belong to everybody although everybody has it inside. As long as you are not in the highest states of consciousness, you cannot have this cow."

The king replied, "Don't talk like that. I can have whatever I want because I am the king." He ordered his commander in chief to move the cow. But when the commander in chief went near the cow, the saint whispered in her ear, "Mother, I cannot take care of you now. Please protect yourself." Immediately divine people came out from the cow and started fighting. They defeated all the soldiers including the king and tied their hands behind their backs.

They brought the king in front of the saint and said, "Sir, you taught this man, his father, and even his grandfather, but even then he insulted you. Tell us what punishment we should give him."

The saint said, "He is like my grandson. How can I punish him? He is just foolish, that's all. Leave him." The saint excused them all and they were freed.

The king humbly asked the saint, "Father, nothing fascinates me more than this cow. Please tell me how to get it."

The saint said, "Leave the kingdom. Become a saint, evolve, and activate your chakras. When you have activated the soma chakra you will get this cow."* King Vishvamitra followed that advice for the rest of his life. He changed from a powerful king into a great saint, who one day had his own wish-fulfilling cow.

———◆———

Desire and Discipline

Desire is the motivating force. If there were no desire we would not be here. Desires are infinite. We always have had and always will have desires. They bring us back to this theater on Earth. This world is the desire of the one who said, "Let there be light," so he is responsible for it. If it destroys itself, he is responsible, not me. But we desire to remain for a long time on planet Earth in a better way, so we talk about violence and ecology.

Desires belong to the body, not to the Self. Self is always seated in bliss (*ananda*) and it has no desires. All desires spring from a contact of mind with the outer world. Desires are produced by objects of desire, but ego feels attached or not. When ego feels attached then it is motivated to fulfill the desire, otherwise ego does not care about it.

Desires are like seeds that will sprout and grow when circumstance are right. But when a seed has been roasted it cannot sprout anymore. By doing penance and hard work you can roast the seeds of desire and then they will not grow anymore. One form of penance is fasting, which is denying yourself some things that you think are necessary for you. I do it an easy way. When I need cold water, I drink hot. When I need a soft bed, I choose a hard one. When I need to stay home, I travel abroad. When I need

*The chakras are subtle energy centers located in the spine and each is associated with specific desires and activities. Certain yogic practices activate the energy (*kundalini*) that usually lies dormant in the lowest chakra (the *muladhara*), allowing it to rise through the chakras, which brings with it inner growth and realization. The soma chakra is located in the forehead. The artistic rendering of the soma chakra in *Chakras, Energy Centers of Transformation,* includes a depiction of Kamadhenu.

not to talk, I speak. So everything that I do is what I don't need to do. That's how I do not do what I need, so I don't need anything. First practice that. Whenever you are craving sugar, eat peppers and burn your tongue.

All disciplines are intended to create more willpower so that you can overrule your ego. If there were no ego then no sadhana—no fasting, no disciplines—would be needed.

5
Curses and Promises

One story that is not included in the abridged versions of Mahabharata is about the eight Vasus, celestial energies guarding the eight directions on Earth: north, south, east, west, and northeast, northwest, southeast, and southwest. Their story explains the birth of the most important character in the main story of the Mahabharata.

The Curse of the Vasus

One day in Dvapara Yuga, the Vasus wanted to spend a holiday on Earth with their spouses. They selected a remote area and went there together. While bathing in a nice river, they played games, throwing water over each other, and enjoying their holiday. They thought they were in a deserted place and they did not know that Saint Vasishta was living there with his beautiful wish-fulfilling cow Kamadhenu. The saint had gone to collect some wood for the evening prayers, leaving the cow near the river.

When the group came out of the water one of the ladies felt like having something warm and said, "Oh it would be nice to have a hot tea." The cow heard it and immediately a glass full of nice warm tea appeared. The lady took the glass and drank it. The tea had a divine taste, which she never had tasted before. She said to her husband, "This cow is great; you ask something and then she provides you with the best quality. Let's take her home."

The husband replied, *"We cannot just take this cow home. The owner of this cow must be somewhere nearby."*

But sometimes if a lady likes something she wants to have it, no matter whether it is right or wrong. So she said, *"Come on, you say you love me but you can't even do this much for me? Can't you take this cow back home?"*

The husband felt he had to prove his love for her and said, *"Okay, honey, I'll take it for you. But when the owner finds out his cow is gone, he will create problems."*

The lady said, *"You are afraid of nothing. Everything is okay. Let's take it."*

The husband gave in and all of the Vasus got involved. Seven of them were on the lookout to help the one who untied the rope of the cow and led her away.

Then the saint came home and saw his precious cow being taken away. He closed his eyes and said, *"Mother what is happening to you? Please help yourself and come to me."* When fulfilling a wish the cow first produces the requirements needed to fulfill the wish, so out of the cow came armed people who liberated the cow and then disappeared again.

The Vasus felt guilty and they were afraid the saint would curse them, so they wanted to apologize. The saint said, *"Why are you taking my cow away? You are divine guardians of the planet. You should not do this."*

They said, *"It is such a marvelous cow. We did not really intend to steal the cow, but our wives persuaded us."*

The saint said, *"I have heard this story many times before and it is wrong. Don't blame your wives. If you don't want to do something wrong you will not do it even if god wants you to. It was you who did it. You can earn Kamadhenu by working with yourself and generating that energy within you but not by stealing. You are celestial beings living in heaven, but for this act I curse you to incarnate on Earth because that is the place where everybody has to come to pay back their karmas. You have to be born as humans with five sense organs and five work organs. Then you will suffer from the tortures that come to you by not getting your needs and desires fulfilled."*

One of the Vasus objected, *"But Sir, I was only supporting."*

Another said, "I only showed the cow a piece of grass so that she would follow us. There is the one who actually stole the cow and it was his wife who inspired him."

Saint Vasishta said, "I can excuse you, but you will have to bear some of the karma that you have created. The seven who were only helping to steal the cow without touching her will have to remain on Earth just for a short period of time. But the one who untied the rope and actually took the cow will have to live on Earth for a longer period of time."

The holiday was over and the Vasus went back to their abode. They worried, "When will I take birth? How will I take birth? Where will I take birth? What will happen?" They had never been incarnated as humans before and they were afraid of Earth because it is a place of confusion, darkness, violence, aggression, and indiscipline.

———◆———

The Origin of Ganga

Many stories are told about the origin of Ganga and this is the most famous one.

❦

Bali and the Dwarf

Once upon a time the demon King Bali had become very powerful. He occupied Earth, underworld, and heaven, so he possessed all. The gods in heaven and the humans on Earth started complaining to Vishnu, the god of preservation. They asked him to break the dominance of the demonic forces. Vishnu agreed and he incarnated as a dwarf. He went to King Bali and said, "I am a little brahmin doing sadhana. I would like to make a hut somewhere so I need some land."

King Bali had taken a vow that if any beggar came and asked for anything, he would give it. So he agreed to give the amount of land measured by three steps of the dwarf. Then the dwarf grew gigantic and in one step he measured the whole earth. In the second step he measured all of space. Then he said, "In two steps I have measured the whole universe, but still I need one more step of land. Now where can I put my foot to make the third step?"

The demon king used to think that he was invincible and that he owned everything so that he could afford to give anybody anything. But that was mere ego and now his ego was broken. He said, "You can put your foot on my head." Then Vishnu put his foot on Bali's head and pushed him down to the underworld where he still lives and rules.

When Vishnu had stepped over the earth and lifted his left foot to step over heaven, the foot reached the place where Brahma, the creator of the world was dwelling. Vishnu had put all his energy in his left foot, like when you pull a rope in a tug of war you put your energy in your hands. Brahma is a grandfather who sometimes thinks about saving for his grandchildren, so when he saw Vishnu's foot, he said to himself, "What a great opportunity to get some of Vishnu's energy." He took his water pot (kamandalu) and washed Vishnu's left big toe. The washing water contained lots of the divine energy of Vishnu, the preserver. Brahma kept it in his water pot for some time and then he gave it the shape of a lady who was called Ganga and lived in heaven.

Ganga's Descent

Here are two little stories that each explain why Ganga had to come to Earth.

Ganga and Durvasa

When Ganga was living in heaven it happened one day that Rishi Durvasa walked by wearing only a small piece of cloth. A gust of wind came and uncovered his private parts. All those present considerately pretended not to have seen anything except for Ganga who started laughing. The saint got angry with her and said, "If you laugh at me I will teach you some manners. For that you have to take birth as a woman on Earth."

Ganga replied, "I am sorry, sir; please do not let me become a mortal woman. That would be too much. I can't do that." The saint calmed a little and said, "Okay, you will be a woman, but you will also be a river and people will worship you as the holy river Ganga."

She said, "If I have to I will go to Earth. But how will I find my way back here where I belong?"

Rishi Durvasa said, "As long as your water remains pure and people can use it, you will remain on Earth. But there will come a time when bad people will extract all the oil from the earth, pollute the air and water, and destroy the environment. Your water also will become impure and when nobody can drink it anymore then you can leave Earth and come back here." Ganga happily agreed because a few thousand human years are just a few seconds to divine beings and she did not mind spending such a little while on Earth as a river.

Ganga and Mahabhisha

King Mahabhisha had died and gone to heaven. One day Lord Indra invited all gods, rishis, and human souls of high caliber to his court. King Mahabhisha accepted the invitation and went to Indra's court. There he saw Ganga for the first time and she was really beautiful. During the meeting a gust of wind came that lifted up her wrap and uncovered her breasts. The gods averted or closed their eyes, but the king stared at Ganga's body. Brahma did not like that a man looked at his daughter in that way. If per chance her body became visible people were supposed to look somewhere else, but this son of a human didn't. Ganga took her time to cover herself, maybe because she was a little bit of an exhibitionist or maybe she wanted to do a little sunbathing. Together they had a game going on with one enjoying showing her body and the other enjoying the view. When a game starts it always should come to an end. Therefore Brahma cursed his daughter and the king to take birth on Earth again and finish their karma. When Ganga begged his

pardon, Brahma promised that she could return after having given birth to
the Vasus.

———◆———

In the next little story Ganga promises the Vasus to help them
incarnate on Earth.

Ganga and the Vasus

The eight Vasus knew about the curse on Ganga. They thought they would
be better off being born from Ganga than from any other woman because
she was holy and her good karma would help them to return to heaven. They
went to Ganga and explained that just like her they also had been cursed
to take birth on Earth. They said, "Mother, like you, we have been cursed to
be born on Earth. Only one of us stole a cow, but the others are innocent
and should not suffer unnecessarily. We ask to take birth from you and then
quickly be released from our bodies so that we can come back here. And the
one who has to live a full life also would rather take birth from you than
from anybody else."

Ganga agreed to help them. She promised to give birth to them and
that soon after birth she would try to release them, except for the real thief.
That way the seven helpers would be able to return to heaven after nine
months of imprisonment on Earth, but the eighth Vasu would have to suffer
a long life.

———◆———

PART TWO

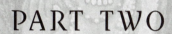

The Story of "Great India"

6

Shantanu, Ganga, and the Birth of Bhishma

The central action of the Mahabharata begins with Ganga's decision that the time had come for her to go to Earth to bear the children of Shantanu, king of Hastinapura. He was a brave and nice king, but he was full of lust, which caused events with elaborate consequences.

Shantanu's Fascination and Its Deadly Repercussions

One day Shantanu was walking along the bank of river Ganga thinking, "I am young, I am a king, I have everything, but I am not married. My life would be better if I had a good wife by my side." To his astonishment, he saw a beautiful lady coming out of the river. It was Ganga who appeared to Shantanu as a lady. She could stay inside the river Ganga because the river was her outer body. But she could also change form and appear as a beautiful woman or anything she liked.

Immediately King Shantanu was fascinated by the beauty and charm of the lady. He approached her to enjoy her beauty and ask her name. She told him her name was Ganga. He asked, "I am amazed seeing you come out of the water. How is that possible?"

She said, "Don't ask me. I can't tell you that."

Sometimes a person becomes so fascinated by another that he or she wants to win the other at any cost. The more the other resists, the more persistent the person becomes.

The king was so fascinated by Ganga's beauty that he wanted to marry her. He said, "Well, whoever you are, you are beautiful and I would like to marry you."

She said, "No, that is not possible, you can't marry me."

He said, "I am the king of this country and I am single. I have a kingdom, wealth, soldiers. I have merits, I am a great warrior, I am known throughout the country, why can't you marry me?"

Ganga said, "I would like to marry you but there are problems."

He said, "I don't care about any problem."

This is everybody's story: when you marry a person, you also marry all the problems of the person. And after marriage you don't see the person anymore, but you only see the problems.

Ganga told Shantanu, "I cannot marry you because I am never constant. All the time I am flowing from here to there to there."

Shantanu replied, "So you are not constant, but if you can stay with me it will be paradise."

She said, "I can stay with you, but after a few years I will have to go away."

The king protested, "Once we are married we will live together. You just cannot go like that. I cannot live without you."

She said, "Marriage is a serious matter. I need to prepare myself to answer your question. Please give me some time. We can meet here again tomorrow and then I will give you my answer."

Because of her promise to the Vasus, Ganga had to find a husband who would tolerate her killing her newborn babies. I don't think any man could tolerate that. It was difficult to find a man who was stupid enough, so she needed to become so attractive that the king would be blind with love and accept all her conditions. She wanted to bring Shantanu to the boiling point so that he would accept anything. That was the real reason for asking him to come back the next day.

Shantanu impatiently asked, "Why tomorrow? Why not today?"

She said, "Because I need some time to think."

The king agreed to come back the next day. He went home, but he could not eat anything and at night he could not sleep. All night he was lying on his bed thinking about the lady who emerged out of the river. Her beauty was not from this world. The more the king thought about her, the more stupid he got.

This is always the case. When you think too much about somebody then the person in your fantasy becomes more real and the real person becomes a stranger. King Shantanu got completely entangled in his fantasy.

Next day the king went to the river again and the lady was there. Again he asked her to marry him. She said, "I can marry you and live with you only if you allow me to do whatever I want without questioning my conduct and without interfering. The minute you ask me to explain myself I will leave you. Do you promise never to ask me about my past, where I come from, whose daughter I am, and what my heritage is, never to object what I do, and never to stop me from doing whatever I am doing?"

Blinded by passion, Shantanu agreed. He said, "I promise I will never ask you anything and I will never object or question you. I will never talk to you badly and always let you do what you want. You are allowed to be free and do anything you want. Now will you marry me?"

Shantanu did not think that the consequences of his actions could be far-reaching; he was mad and he just wanted her in his bed. That is why he is a symbol of passion. Maybe this was the most stupid decision of King Shantanu, but without it the story of Mahabharata would not be there. Ganga needed a stupid person and this one was stupid enough, so she agreed to marry him. Everybody wants to marry a person who is ready to accept all their weaknesses and problems without being disturbed. But it is difficult to find such an ideal husband who will not bother you.

The king didn't know about the curse of the eight Vasus who had to be conceived and hang upside down for nine months in that ocean of soothing vibrations as people call it or in hell as we call it. He didn't know that Ganga had promised to return seven of them to heaven as soon as possible after they were born.

Shantanu and Ganga married immediately and started living together. The king was happy to have such a beautiful wife. She was also holy because she was mother Ganga and she knew all the scriptures. She would chant beautiful things and the palace became a paradise. Everybody around was enchanted.

Soon Ganga became pregnant. The king was exuberant when the baby was born, but Ganga had the problem of how to release the newborn baby from its body. Normally a disease is required for that to happen, but the baby was healthy. There were no chemicals available for a capsule or an injection. Ganga chose an organic method; it was the only one she could think of. She took the baby to the river and threw it in the water.

One of the ladies from the palace brought the king the news that a son had been born and the next minute another lady came to tell that the baby had been thrown in the river. The king was horrified and shocked. He had never imagined that a mother could do that. Everybody expects a mother to cherish her child, to nourish and to save the child, but not this mother. All the people of the town were talking about it. "We have never seen a mother who kills her own child. What kind of mother is this?"

The king could not do anything because of his stupid vow not to question her conduct and not to interfere. He had to live with her, appreciate her, and make love to her. A year passed by with singing, dancing, drinking, eating, and having holidays. The queen got pregnant again and she gave birth to another child. Again she got up, took up the child, and walked toward the river. The king said to himself, "Oh god, she is going to do the same thing again." But he was bound by his words and he couldn't say anything. Again she threw the child into the river; finished. Who could have tolerated it twice? But King Shantanu was so madly in love with lady Ganga that he could.

People started saying, "What kind of queen is this? She kills her own children. She must be a witch or something awful." But they respected and loved their king so much that they did not want to rebel against him. Also it did not concern them because it was a personal affair of the king.

Seven children were born and all seven were thrown into the river and drowned. With the third child the king followed the mother a few steps and then realized he could not do anything. With the fourth child he walked a long distance and considered stopping his wife, but he thought of his promise never to interfere with her affairs and returned home. With the fifth child he went up to the bank of the river and while she was throwing the child, he considered stopping her. Every time the king went a step farther, but he was bound by his foolish vow and he could not object. Losing seven children this way almost drove him crazy.

——————◆——————

Shantanu symbolizes the weaker side of human nature. He represents lust and passion. His story shows that when we are caught by lust we become dumb and we let wrong things happen in front of our eyes without protest. The king was powerful and he could order any person to do anything, but here he was helpless before his wife and he could not even ask her why she was doing such horrible things. He had no determination; he only had consideration and tolerance for that lady. I call him a coward because he allowed his wife to kill seven children.

The Birth of Bhishma

After the death of his seventh son the king said to himself, "Next time I will stop her. Let her go away, but I want to save my child." Again his wife became pregnant and again a son was born. When Ganga picked up the baby to throw *it into the river, the king stopped her and said, "What are you doing? I forbid you to destroy this child. Eight times I have become a father and now I want to keep this one son."*

She said, "I was loving you and living with you and I gave birth eight times without objecting.* You promised me you would never ask me why I was doing anything. Also I told you that the day you asked me this question I would leave you. So now that you have broken your promise it is time for me to leave."

Then she told him about the eight Vasus who had tried to steal Kamadhenu from Vasishta and been cursed by him to incarnate on Earth and her promise to liberate them. She said, "Seven Vasus were only helpers so their punishment was to be born as human beings and after a few minutes be free again. But this one was the actual culprit who has to live a long life. Now I am taking him with me because no father can take care of a child like the mother can. I promise I will bring him back to you when he has completed his education and can take care of himself. He will be safe and he will become your legal heir. By keeping him you lose me." Then the lady stepped into the river and disappeared with the baby. She took the baby to heaven.

King Shantanu went home. He started feeling terribly lonely, worse than if he had remained unmarried. He was very sad and he felt that his life was meaningless because he was a king without a queen, nobody to communicate with, nobody taking care of him. He got restless and used to roam along the bank of the river Ganga. He was not going anywhere. In fact he was just waiting for Ganga to come out of the water so that he could talk to her.

———◆———

A side story is that one day when Shantanu was roaming around he came across two newborn babies lying on a deerskin. One was a boy and the other a girl. Shantanu brought them to the teacher of the family and told him to take care of them. Because they had come by the grace of god the boy was called Kripa (meaning "grace, benevolence")

---

*Most modern women would not like to give birth eight times.

and the girl Kripi. They also play significant roles later on in the story of the Mahabharata.

Meanwhile Bhishma grew up in heaven. As a boy he was educated about dharma, scriptures, and martial arts by the highest gurus such as the god Shiva, Sage Vasishta, Brihaspati (Jupiter), and Parashurama, the sixth incarnation of Vishnu the preserver (after the dwarf incarnation). Parashurama was a savage man with an axe, famous for his power and his furious nature. He was the best archer and the best teacher of martial arts. His name is mentioned in the Mahabharata several times, but he is also mentioned in the Ramayana. He became angry with Rama when he had broken the bow of Shiva and he was only pacified when Rama showed him who he really was (the seventh incarnation of Vishnu).

Bhishma's Return

Every day Shantanu would go to the spot on the bank of the river where Ganga had disappeared and sit down. He used to say things like, "I would like to see you. I forgive you for what you did. Please come back to me." But nothing happened. Only after fourteen years, when Bhishma no longer needed his mother and his education was complete, did the time come for him to return to Earth. The king was sitting near the river when he saw a young boy coming out of the water and going back again. He was wondering how the boy could stay under water. Then the boy came out again with a bow and arrow in his hands. He chanted a mantra and shot the arrow up. Thousands of arrows came and went into the river so close to each other that they blocked the passage of the water. The king was astonished.

Then Ganga came out of the water just like the day when they first met. She said, "I bring back your son; his name is Devadatta (gift of god). I have taken proper care of him and he has been educated by the best teachers. He learned all the scriptures from saints and knows all about dharma. He is well versed in archery and all the other martial arts by the great sage Parashurama. He knows everything a king should know. He is capable of being the legal heir of your throne and kingdom."

King Shantanu said, "Good that you brought him back. Now please come and live with me."

She said, "I did not come here to live with you but only to return your son. We will never meet again."

She went away and the king went home with his son. He was happy to have such a great son after all those years and he loved him very much. He was such a handsome prince, elegant, well behaved, and well educated. The town and the whole kingdom of Hastinapura were happy with the son of King Shantanu and his wife Ganga. He was strong, well versed in the scriptures, and well trained in martial arts.

———◆———

Devadatta, son of Shantanu and Ganga, is the central character of Mahabharata, though he is best known by the name he came to have later, Bhishma. When Ganga took him to heaven she made him a fatherless child. According to dharma a child should remain with both mother and father. By returning the son to his father only after fourteen years even Ganga was not following dharma. Similarly Buddha was not following dharma when he left his wife and child to run away and become an ascetic.

7

Satyavati, Shantanu, and Bhishma's Terrible Vow

The Mahabharata shows that events or people who initially seem insignificant can have a great impact over time. One person with lowly beginnings who became central to the story of the Mahabharata was Satyavati.

Birth of Vyasa

A fisherman was living with his wife and their young daughter near the river Yamuna. The daughter was beautiful, but she had the disadvantage of smelling like fish. That's why she was called Matsyagandha (matsya means "fish" and gandha means "smell" or "fragrance"). When the fisherman was busy on the land and did not need his boat, the girl used to sit on the bank of the river waiting for passengers to take across the river for a penny.

One day Parashara came. He was a grandson of Vasishta and a saint and rishi who had done lots of penance and had acquired great powers. He asked the girl to take him across the river. She asked him to sit down in the boat, but when he did he was horrified by her smell. He was a strict vegetarian who never had eaten or prepared any fish in his life. When he protested she excused herself and said she could not help it because she was living in a fisherman's house surrounded by fish.

The rishi knew that crossing the river would take a long time. The boat was made from a hollow tree and it had a sail but no motor, chain, or helm. To reach the other side of the river they had to start upstream at an angle and in the middle change direction. He decided to change the body chemistry of the girl and make her smell good. He took some water in his hand, chanted a mantra, sprinkled some water on her, and said, "Smell like jasmine." Immediately the body of the girl changed and a nice fragrance of jasmine flowers started coming from her body. After this incident her name became Pushpagandha, "the one who smells like a flower." Later she became known as Satyavati.

The rishi had forgotten that bad things sometimes are good. As long as the girl smelled like fish he kept at a distance, but when she smelled like jasmine flowers, the rishi felt attracted. The girl said, "You are full of magical powers. Can you tell me my future?"

The rishi closed his eyes, visualized, and said, "Future is expecting a lot from you."

She said, "I am just the daughter of a fisherman. How can future want something from me?"

He said, "That I don't know. I only know that you were not born to take people across the river. You are supposed to be a queen (maharani) and a lot will depend on you. In the future you will need help, and I would like to give you a son who will help you through."

She said, "But I am unmarried, a virgin, how can I get a son from you?"

He said, "You don't have to bear the son. Just think that you conceive my child and then you will give birth to the child immediately, but your body will remain unchanged."

She said, "And then, how can I take care of a child back home when I am not married?" He said, "You don't have to. I will take him with me and take care of him. I will teach him, give him the education of the scriptures, and make him a saint. In the future he will help you and your family."

She agreed, "If I remain a virgin and don't have to take the burden of *carrying the child and don't need to do anything, then I am ready to have your child."*

The rishi asked her to close her eyes. He did some energy play and when she opened her eyes, she saw a beautiful black child in her lap. Because of his beautiful dark skin, he got the name Krishna (meaning "dark") and because he was born on an island in a river, he received the name Dvaipayana (meaning "two streams"). So his full name was Krishna Dvaipayana "the dark boy from the two streams." As agreed the rishi went away with the child. When the girl came back home, she did not tell anybody she had a son and she even almost forgot. But one day she would be the queen of India and remember him again.

Rishi Parashara took the child to the forest. The son never lived with the mother.* The rishi took good care of him and taught him all his knowledge. When he had become a storyteller he received the name Vyasa, which means "one who narrates scriptures."

———◆———

When talking about a scripture I am performing the job of a *vyasa*. When a religious festival is arranged we prepare a seat for a vyasa, a person who will sit on it and talk about scriptures. Krishna Dvaipayana Vyasa became the greatest writer of his time, who even composed the Mahabharata in which his own story is narrated. Because he compiled the Vedas and gave discourses about them, he was also called Vedavyasa.

☙❦❧

Shantanu Becomes Fascinated Again

After Ganga had left, King Shantanu had no wife, which made him very sad.† One day he was wandering around and he had to cross the river Yamuna near the place where the fisherman and his family were living. There he met

---

*Usually children growing up without a mother or a father suffer from a complex and need therapy but not this boy.

†At that time there were no therapists, otherwise he would surely have gone for therapy.

the girl who smelled like flowers, and he asked her to take him across. He didn't have to cross the river, but he just wanted her company.

When they reached the other bank she said, "Okay sir, now we have reached the other side, so you can get down."

Then he asked her to take him back again, so she did. When she had taken him back and forth several times, the girl asked, "You are neither going this way nor that way. All the time you are roaming on the water with me. What do you want?"

He said, "Don't you understand what I want?"

She said, "Yes, in a way I understand what you want, otherwise I would not have taken you across so many times. But please now tell me clearly." Shantanu was old enough to be her father, but when he sat in the boat the fragrance of jasmine and the fragrance of youth had intoxicated him so much that he said, "I am a king, but I have nobody. I like your smell and I like you, and I would like to marry you. Will you marry me?"

She said, "I cannot answer this question myself because I need the permission of my father to marry you. So please ask my father."

When two partners feel like marrying and all is okay, they can decide for themselves. If King Shantanu had not already had a son, then Pushpagandha would have married him without any problem. But everybody in the kingdom knew that the king had a son, so not all was okay and negotiations were needed to arrange the marriage.

The king went to the father of the girl. The fisherman was honored by the visit of the king. He said, "Sir, I am honored by your visit, and I would like to serve you. Please tell me what you want."

The king said, "I would like to marry your daughter."

The fisherman was really a shrewd dealer. He said, "I am just a poor fisherman and a boatman. I cannot find a better match for my daughter than you. I would like to marry my daughter to a king and have her child one day become king. The children of my daughter should inherit all the belongings of her husband. But the problem is that you have a grown-up son with the status *of crown prince. He is the legal heir to your kingdom, so my daughter will only live like a slave in your house and a child of hers will never be king. Such a marriage I oppose. Only if you deprive your son of the right to inherit the kingdom after your death will I marry my daughter to you."*

King Shantanu got really nervous. After many years of waiting he had recently got his son from his beloved wife Ganga. And because he loved his son he could not send him out of his kingdom in order to enjoy being the husband of the fisherman's daughter and let her children rule the kingdom of Hastinapura. He said, "That is impossible. I love my son very much. He is well educated and strong. In every way he is capable to become king and save the kingdom. I cannot disinherit him from the kingdom."

He returned to the palace. But he was a passionate person and he could not sleep. He had fallen in love with the girl, and he could only think about her, but on the other hand he loved his son very much. He was torn in two and became depressed. In the following months he became thin and weak. He had signs of a hidden sickness. All the time he was thinking about that lady who smelled like jasmine flowers. All the time he was sad and he stopped taking care of the kingdom. He was sitting in a tent near the river watching Pushpagandha rowing the boat across the river.

Bhishma's Vows

Bhishma saw his father getting more sick and weak every day and he searched to find the reason for it. One of the ministers told him that his father was in love with the fisherman's daughter and wanted to marry her but the girl's father would not allow it. Actually it was time for Bhishma to marry, but his father was still thinking about marrying so Bhishma could not. The boy did not want to see his father unhappy and thought he would make a sacrifice and try to persuade the fisherman to allow the marriage.

Bhishma went to the fisherman, introduced himself, and said, "Please marry your daughter to my father, otherwise he will die of sadness."

The fisherman said, "I would like to do that, but the problem is that you are the eldest son and you will be the king, not my daughter's children. I want my grandchildren to inherit the throne."

Then Bhishma made a solemn vow. He said, "I give you my word that I renounce the throne and will never claim the kingdom so that the children of your daughter will be the legal heirs of the kingdom. You can be sure that your grandchild will become king. Now you should have no problem and you should marry your daughter to my father."

The fisherman said, "I honor your words and I believe you. You are great. You have made a vow not to take the kingdom. But what will happen if you marry and have children? One day they may stand up and say that their grandfather was a little crazy to marry a young girl and give the rights to the kingdom to her progeny. They will say that the kingdom actually belonged to their father and they inherited it. Then they will fight to get the kingdom and my grandchildren will suffer. Therefore I cannot marry my daughter to your father."

Bhishma said, "For that I also have a solution. I take a vow that I will remain a celibate for the rest of my life. I will never marry and never have children. So the kingdom will have no other legal heirs. That way the progeny of your daughter will safely enjoy the kingdom of Hastinapura. Now you should be satisfied and marry your daughter to my father."

All of the fisherman's conditions had been met, and he agreed to marry his daughter to King Shantanu.

When you are so full of youth it is very difficult to decide to be a brahmachari and not to marry. These days it is easy, and I see lots of people everywhere who are not married. But at that time it was difficult because a brahmachari was really a brahmachari. The real name of the prince was Devadatta (gift of god), but because of his vow, which was so very hard to follow, the people of the kingdom gave him the title "Bhishma" meaning "one who performs a terrible vow." But he called himself Gangaputra, son of Ganga, or Bharata, member of the clan of Bharata, because he was a descendant from the Bharata who once was such a great king of India that Bharata became another name for India.

By his vow to remain celibate all his life, Bhishma sacrificed his life and pleasure to the kingdom. All his life he did not enjoy any sexual pleasure and he did not show any sign of being a male. He was a humble person, had no relationships, and he aimed at developing higher consciousness.

Bhishma brought the girl to his father and said, "Father here is the lady whom you want so much. Marry her and live with her in peace. I don't want to see you sad."

The father was astonished and said, "How can you do that? You are the one who will be the king after me. I have made you the crown prince."

The son said, "Yes but I have taken a vow never to claim the kingdom and never to have any children that can claim the kingdom."

The king said, "But why did you unnecessarily do such a sacrifice for me? I am an old man and I have already enjoyed life. I don't need to enjoy life more. I could live like this and I could have forgotten this woman. But you have not seen the world. You are a young man who just came to the world and then you renounce having a woman in your life. I don't like that you deprive yourself of the best thing you can do in your life."

The son said, "I already have done it, so now there is no going back and you have to marry her."

The father was overwhelmed by the sacrifice. He said, "I want to reward you for doing such a big sacrifice for me. I give you a boon that you will be able to select the time of your death. You will not die as long as you do not decide to die and as long as you are not ready to die, nobody and nothing can kill you; no man, no divine power, and no weapon. Only if you are prepared to die can death come near you." That boon made Bhishma fearless because nobody could kill him unless he permitted it. That made him even more powerful.

Shantanu and Satyavati married and they had two sons: Chitrangada and Vicitravirya. When they were nine and ten years old, Shantanu died. The boys were dependable and a little weak. Bhishma promised his father on his deathbed that he would take care of the kingdom of Hastinapura at all costs; he pledged to never desert it and always be a humble servant of the one on the throne.

———◆———

8

Tangled Dynasty

In the old days India consisted of many small states ruled by different kings. In the northwest was the kingdom of Gandhara (or Kandahar in Persian), which is now a part of Afghanistan. In the northeast was the kingdom of Panchala. Benares, Bengal, Bihar, and Rajasthan were separate kingdoms. Some were ruled by important kings, such as Jarasandha or Sishupala, who are often mentioned in the Mahabharata and the Srimad Bhagavata Purana.

Hastinapura was ruled by the descendents of Kuru, who were esteemed to be highly religious and followers of dharma. Several kingdoms neighbored Hastinapura, which was in the area that is now Old Delhi and Haryana. To the east was the kingdom of Pataliputra or Patna where Buddha came from. To the north was Chakushan and other dynasties. In the south was Mathura, the powerful kingdom of the fearless cow-herding Abhira tribe ruled by King Ugrasena, the maternal grandfather of Krishna.

When a king wanted to prove his supremacy over other kings, he would first perform a particular ritual and then start to annex the kingdoms in all directions through what was known as *digvijaya*. This meant that the king would go around with his army along the borders of his territory, trying to subdue any neighboring king that did not accept his supremacy. If a neighboring king brought gifts and offered his friendship then the friendship was immediately accepted and no fight was needed. All befriended kings were obliged to attend meetings arranged by the supreme king and to bring him gifts. Also they had to help if a calamity happened or in case of war.

Because of his celibacy Bhishma had much energy to spend, and he used it to expand the kingdom of Hastinapura. When you can't marry you conquer kingdoms. It is a way to waste energy, but it is less consuming than being married. Those who are married understand me. Fighting a war outside was easier than having a war at home because the outside war was from sunrise to sunset whereas the war at home never ends. So Bhishma organized the army and started conquering kingdoms all around. By subduing the neighboring kings, he made the kingdom of Hastinapura more glorious. If a kingdom resisted, he conquered it only to give it back and charge some small taxes. That way he succeeded in befriending all the neighboring kingdoms.

Bhishma was much like the Dutch men that I saw when I came to Holland for the first time and I was going through a canal. They were sitting on the shore with their rods and lines. When I asked them why they were fishing with so much fish available in the market, they replied, "We don't eat these fish. We only teach them not to get caught." So first they would catch the fish on the hook and pull it out of the water. Then they would take it off the hook and put it back in the water so that it wouldn't come near a hook anymore. They did not really harm the fish. Similarly Bhishma did not really harm the kings. The fighting was rather to subdue the ego and create friendship than to shed blood.

Bhishma and Amba

After the death of King Shantanu, his eldest son Chitrangada became the king, but he ruled the kingdom only in name. Actually the supreme power of Hastinapura was in the hands of queen Satyavati. Bhishma obediently carried out her orders and treated her like his real mother. As he had been educated in heaven, Bhishma knew all martial arts and divine weapons. He was so strong that when his stepbrothers Chitrangada and Vicitravirya had become men who were able take care of the kingdom, they could spend most of their time enjoying ladies and playing games.

But then Chitrangada got killed in a battle with the king of the Gandharva tribe. Vicitravirya was installed on the throne. To find a bride for him, Bhishma went to a svayamvara* that was organized by the king of Benares (Kashi) who was a sincere follower of dharma. His three daughters Amba, Ambika, and Ambalika were going to freely choose their husbands at the gathering in the royal court.

Amba was already having an affair with Salva the king of Saubha and her marriage was almost settled. At the svayamvara she was surely planning to choose Salva. When Bhishma appeared at the svayamvara, he challenged everybody. King Salva did not accept Bhishma's supremacy, but he was defeated by Bhishma and his army. On Amba's request Bhishma released him. Then Bhishma brought the three princesses to Hastinapura. Amba explained her situation to Bhishma and asked permission to return to her fiancé, which Bhishma allowed. But when Amba met King Salva, he rejected her because she had been taken away by force and then given back like alms to a beggar, which his pride could not bear. Then Amba returned to Bhishma and told her misfortune. Bhishma said he could teach him a lesson, but he could not make him marry her. So Amba had nowhere to go. She wanted to marry either her fiancé or Bhishma who had taken her and nobody else. But her fiancé refused to take her back and Bhishma was not a man.

Amba became frustrated and angry. She took shelter with Parashurama, the teacher of Bhishma, but he also said he could not help her because even he could not defeat Bhishma. Then Amba started performing severe penances. Determined to take revenge on Bhishma, she left her body, to take birth again as warrior Shikandin. Many years later she finally would have her way. From

*Svayam means "self" and vara means "choosing." In ancient India svayamvara was a practice in which a woman of marriageable age chose her husband herself from a group of suitors, often after he had proved himself by winning some competition.

the day that Amba was rejected by her fiancé until the day that she could shoot Bhishma, she only wanted to take revenge on Bhishma.

Revenge is a basic problem of Kali Yuga. Even after the death of the body, Amba's revenge continued and that is very bad. In my book on numerology* I explain that revenge is a pet word for number 8 people and that their karmic lesson is learning to forgive.

⚬❦⚬

Vyasa Fathers Three Sons

Amba's sisters Ambika and Ambalika married Vicitravirya, but shortly after the marriage Vicitravirya died of tuberculosis without leaving any progeny. The big kingdom of Hastinapura was in a crisis. Satyavati's father had arranged that her children would have all the rights to the kingdom of Hastinapura, but now both her sons had died without progeny and there was nobody to claim the kingdom. There was a strong caretaker of the kingdom and two widows in the house but no legal heir.

Queen Satyavati approached Bhishma who was taking care of the kingdom just like a true king. She said, "The time has come that you should break your vow and marry to father a legal heir to the throne of the kingdom."

Bhishma refused, saying, "I have taken a vow to remain celibate, and I will not break it. I cannot help you."

She asked, "If you are not going to help then how will the kingdom of Hastinapura survive?"

He said, "I don't know; only time can solve the problem."

Satyavati became desperate and she worried what would happen with the family and with the world. Then she remembered her son Vyasa who had been born when she met the maharishi Parashara before her marriage with King Shantanu. Vyasa was now a full-fledged saint and saints can make the impossible possible. He was related by blood with the two sons who had

---

Numerology, with Tantra, Ayurveda, and Astrology (Rochester, Vt.: Destiny Books, 1995).

died. Maybe Vyasa could help her by impregnating her two daughters-in-law who were still there. It is hard for a mother to reveal having a son before she got married, but in a time of emergency, people put their shame aside. So Satyavati told Bhishma about Vyasa and she asked him to go and bring Vyasa to the palace. Maybe he would save the dynasty.

Bhishma obeyed the order of his stepmother. He went to Vyasa and asked him to come with him to the royal palace. When they arrived, Vyasa touched the feet of his mother and asked, "Mother, why have you called me?"

She said, "The kingdom is without a legal heir and my two daughters-in-law are widows. The throne should not remain empty for a long time, so we have to do something. Please use your psychic power (siddhi) to give a child to each of the two ladies so that the kingdom will have a legal heir."

In those days yogis were following the law of brahmacharya strictly, so they did not indulge in physical activity, but the scriptures allowed immaculate conception (niyoga). When two persons unite it is yoga (union), but when a child is conceived without physical union it is called niyoga. When a queen did not have progeny because the king was not fertile or because the king had died, then the scriptures allowed the queen to conceive a child with the help of a yogi if he would consent to pass his energy to her without physical contact. The yogi would sit down in meditation, producing an energy field, and any lady entering that field would conceive a child. This way the queen could give birth to a legal heir and save the kingdom. It was possible in those days and it is possible still, but nowadays yogis are not doing that anymore because there are other possibilities.

Vyasa had been doing tapasya (austerity or penance), so he looked ferocious like a cave man. He said, "At this moment my face is wild and it will be difficult for the ladies to bear my radiance and accept me. If you give me a few days to become quiet and calm then I will look more pleasant and the ladies can see me and have beautiful children in a right way."

But Satyavati was impatient and the queens were in their fertile part of their cycle, so she thought there was no time to waste. She wanted Vyasa to immediately impregnate the queens Ambika and Ambalika. Patience is a sign of strength in dharma. The more strength you have in following dharma, the more patience you have and the more deeply your prayers influence the environment and the world. But when dharma is weak, people become impatient. Satyavati said there was no time to waste and she insisted until Vyasa gave in.

Satyavati summoned Ambika and Ambalika and told them to undress. They had to enter the room where the maharishi was sitting in meditation, walk in front of the saint, and then leave. When queen Ambalika had taken off her clothes and entered the room, she saw a man who looked wild. He was radiating so much light that she could not bear it. She got so scared that she closed her eyes and covered them with her hands. Vyasa transferred his energy, but he was not satisfied. When he came out of the room, Satyavati asked what had happened and he said, "The lady is pregnant, but because she could not bear my presence, she closed her eyes and the child will be blind."

She said, "Well, let's try the next one." When queen Ambika entered the room and saw Vyasa, she became yellow with fear. Again the saint was not satisfied. When his mother asked what had happened, he said, "Well, she is pregnant, but as she became yellow the child will be born with jaundice. He will be yellow and his health will not be good."

Satyavati went to the first lady and said, "Because you closed your eyes your son will be blind. Maybe you should try once more so that you can receive a healthy child." But she refused because she could not bear the radiance.

The ladies suggested sending the maidservant who they had brought with them from their mother's house. The maidservant agreed. She thought, "While Vyasa is busy distributing children why shouldn't I also get one?" She undressed, entered the room, and passed by the saint. She was neither afraid nor puzzled. She did not close her eyes nor become yellow. When Vyasa looked at her she confronted him and gave him a good smile. When Vyasa came out of the room, Satyavati inquired what had happened. He said, "The lady will have a brilliant learned son who will never do anything wrong. His name will be ever remembered in the history of the country."

Saint Vyasa went away to the forest, and after nine months three beautiful children were born in the palace. The first queen who had closed her eyes gave birth to Dhritarashtra who was blind. The second queen who had turned pale *gave birth to Pandu who looked like he had anemia or jaundice, the disease that makes people yellow (pandu means "pale" or "yellow"). And the maid who entered the room after the queens gave birth to a healthy son, Vidura.*

————◆————

Actually the blindness of Dhritarashtra and the poor health of Pandu were caused by the impatience of Satyavati.

The Past Life of Vidura

Dharma, which is the law or binding authority, is also Yama, the lord of death who judges your conduct and gives you your place in heaven or hell. This story is about Yama becoming cursed.

⊙ᛦ☯

Yama Receives a Curse

Long ago Rishi Galab was living in a big mountain cave. He used to sit down in the cave near the entrance, meditating most of the time. One day a group of thieves came and saw the saint sitting inside the cave. They had stolen jewels from the king's palace, but when somebody alarmed the guards they had to run away from the palace, police who came chasing them. The thieves were encircled, so they thought the cave might be a good place to hide. They stored the stolen jewels near the saint and hid themselves in the back of the cave. The saint was in deep meditation and did not notice them.

When the police came they searched the cave and found all the gems and jewels near the saint; he appeared to be the chief of the robbers, who were all sitting like yogis. The police arrested everybody and took them to the court of the king where they were interrogated. The thieves said, "Sir, we are not criminals. We have families that depend on us. We were only hired, but he is the one who gave the instructions."

The saint was still sitting in samadhi, having been carried to the king in that same posture. The king asked, "Why did you do this crime?" The saint did not say anything.

The chief of the police said, "Sire, this man pretends to be meditating, but we found the jewelry right next to him."

The king released the gang members and sentenced "their boss" to hang. So the saint was hung on a gallows tree with a rope around his neck. With a normal person the breathing would be cut off and the person would die. But the saint was still in samadhi, so he was not breathing anyway. He kept on hanging for months, but he did not die.

Every day people came to check him only to find that life was still there. People started wondering what was the matter. The news spread that there was a thief who had been hanged by the king, but he was not dying. People got curious because it was very strange. They all came to see the man that had been hung but stayed alive. Some saints who knew Galab Rishi recognized him. They went to the king and said, "King, you are blinded by your passion and by the wrong evidence that was presented to you. Your policemen are not honest. They did not investigate the matter properly. They just arrested someone, but he is a real saint and he is really in samadhi. The thieves must have found an opportunity to hide in his cave and put the jewels near him because he was in samadhi, but he did not steal nor is he a member of their gang. If you punish somebody who is innocent you will suffer from the wrath of god, so please stop this."

The king got upset. He ran to the gallows tree and he had the saint taken down. The visiting saints started chanting mantras and doing rituals and the consciousness of the rishi slowly came back. When he came to his senses he asked what was the matter. The king folded his hands and said, "Sir, I am terribly sorry. Our police found my jewelry near you, so we thought that you were the chief of the robbers, and because you didn't talk, we hung you. You have been hanging here for five months but you did not die. It became clear that you are a saint and not a thief. This happened to you because of my ignorance. I am so sad. Please excuse me."

The saint said, "I have nothing to say to you because you are stupid and your way of living is stupid. I don't feel bad that you hung me because you did not know me. But this damn god Yama, the judge who is sitting upstairs, I want to ask him why I had to be punished like this."

The saint directly went to Yama (Dharmaraja), the lord of dharma, who is the lord of justice who decides what kind of heaven or hell you should be given for the deeds that you have done in your life. The saint asked him, "Why was I hanged for five months? Why did I have to take this pain although I did not feel it because I was in samadhi?"

Yama answered, "When you were a child you urinated in a hole in which thousands of ants were living. Out of mischief you filled the hole and all the ants died. For that you received this punishment. But because you did not know that so many ants got killed you did not have to suffer the pain of hanging. Because you were in samadhi, nothing happened, so in fact it was a light punishment."

The saint became angry and said, "Dharmaraja, I was an innocent boy. I did it not because of any malicious intention but only because of foolishness and curiosity. For that you gave me such a big punishment? Man does lots of things by his mischievous nature. For example, when people want to tease a person who is sleeping they set fire to a small piece of cotton and put it near the bed so that the sleeper wakes up and they can have a laugh. It is only for fun, but sometimes the bed catches fire and the whole room burns down. Like that accidents happen, but they are not done intentionally."

Yama replied, "When you kill so many, you should be hanged; all ants are living beings, so for killing so many ants you deserved this punishment. If a mistake is there the punishment should be there, whether you do it by mischief or you do it unintentionally."

The saint said, "You are sitting here in heaven writing in everybody's book and deciding about their fate: this one is bad, he must go to hell; that one is good, he can go to heaven. But you don't know everything. As you have never been on Earth you do not know how many things happen by mistake. You don't know how helpless humans are. You don't know how many problems we have inside as well as outside. You do not realize how difficult it is to live on Earth. People who are innocent should not be punished like this.

"So that you will understand, I curse you to be born as a man on Earth. For one lifetime you will be a man and see the nonsense happening in front of your eyes. You will raise your voice to tell everybody the truth, but nobody will *listen to you. Then you will realize human helplessness. You will see that when people are filled with bad vibrations, when they are mischievous and have already planned to do something wrong, they will not listen no matter how much you talk. You won't be able to do anything and you will feel helpless."*

———◆———

Because of this curse, Dharma himself, the lord of justice, had to take birth as a man, Vidura, born from a maidservant. Vidura was pure dharma. He kept on telling everybody about right and wrong, but nobody listened to him. People were so mad, so blinded by their passions and desires, that they ignored his advice. Even when everyone else was convinced that Vidura's advice was correct, still the person involved felt he was right and all others were wrong. Through his incarnation as Vidura, Yama learned that it is difficult to judge what is good and what is bad. There is no use punishing humans because they are not independent and mature enough to be responsible. They are misled by sensations, sense perceptions, desires, and ambitions.

9

The Birth and Abandonment of Karna

Another central character in the Mahabharata is Karna. Once a demon, he incarnated as a demigod who was abandoned by his mother.

❧

Kunti's Mantra and the Sun God

Shurasena, king of the Yadava tribe of brave warriors and cowherds, was living in the area of Mathura and Vrindavan, which is called Brij.* The king had a son called Vasudeva, who later fathered Krishna. He also had a daughter whose name was Pritha, which comes from parthi, *meaning "earth." King Shurasena had a cousin brother,† King Kuntibhoja, who had no offspring. One day Kuntibhoja asked Shurasena for one of his children to love and take care of, and he was allowed to adopt the little girl. Then her name changed from Pritha into Kunti, after the name of her new father.*

When Kunti was about eight years of age Rishi Durvasa visited the palace of King Kuntibhoja. The rishi had a quick temper and therefore he was also

---

*The language spoken there is called Shuraseni and from that came Brij Bhasha, a language related to Hindi.

†In Indian culture cousins are often referred to as "cousin brothers" or "cousin sisters."

known as "the angry rishi." Anything an angry rishi says becomes true, so people were afraid of him and his curses. To avoid becoming cursed, King Kuntibhoja thought he better keep the rishi happy. He asked his daughter to serve the rishi, which she did well in spite of her young age. Normally saints stay no more than three days at one place, but the rishi stayed in the palace for a year. He was happy with Kunti, which is remarkable because making him happy required lots of pleasing things like special food dishes.

When he was about to return to the forest Durvasa said to Kunti, "I am happy with your hard work for me. Ask me for a boon."

Kunti said, "Maharishi, I am just a child and I have all that I need, so I don't have anything to ask for."

He said, "Then I will teach you something that will help you in the future." He could see the future, so he knew the time would come that her husband would not be able to have children. He said, "I will teach you a mantra by which you can receive a son from any god. If you think about any god and chant the mantra, then that god will immediately come to give you a son."

At that time Kunti was still just a child; she did not know about man and woman, babies and motherhood. She only knew that the rishi was happy and wanted to give her something, so she agreed and she learned the mantra. That was a mistake; the rishi should have waited twenty years before giving her the mantra. But he thought he would not be coming back and the girl would need the mantra in the future so he should give it to her right away. After teaching Kunti the mantra he warned her not to recite it unnecessarily and Kunti promised.

After the rishi left, Kunti became curious about whether the mantra really would work. Sometimes doubt came into her mind. Maybe the mantra was not true and maybe the rishi had fooled her just to please her. One day she decided to find out. She looked around and saw the sun shining in the sky and she became fascinated by its beauty. She thought, "Sun is also a god. Why not try and call him?" She took a little water in her hands, looked at the sun, chanted the mantra and sprinkled the water toward the sun.

The whole atmosphere became dark. The rays of the sun separated from the body of the sun and came down to Earth. A figure appeared in front of her, shining like the sun. It was the sun god in human form. She asked, "Who are you?"

The figure replied, "I am Surya. You have just invoked me with your mantra. Here I am, so now ask me for a boon."

She said, "Durvasa Rishi taught me the mantra and I did not know if it would work. I saw you shining and you looked good, so I thought I could try to invoke you. I just wanted to test the mantra. But I really don't need anything. Now that I know the mantra works you can leave."

But when gods come somewhere they cannot leave without giving anything. If the person is caught in any desire they will fulfill it. And if the person has no desire then they can do what they want. Surya said, "I cannot leave like this. I am bound by the power of your mantra and I have to do what the mantra wants me to do, so I have to give you a child."

She said, "But Sir, I am a child and a virgin. I am not married; I can't have a baby. I cannot take care of it. What will I do with a child? I live with my father, and he will be angry with me."

Surya replied, "Until I do what the mantra wants me to do, I cannot leave. So I have to give you a child."

Kunti had no choice.

But Surya also granted her another boon. He said: "You will remain a virgin. The child will find its way through your ear and he will be called Karna (karna means "ear"). He will be born with a natural armor (kavac) that is a part of his body. As long as that armor is on his body no arrow will be able to pierce him and no sword will be able to cut him, so nobody will be able to kill him and he will be invincible. He also will have natural earrings (kundala) made of flesh, which will also be a sign of his being divine and also make him invincible. As long as he has the armor and the earrings, he cannot die."

———◆———

This way of having a baby has big advantages; the child is born without nine months of pregnancy; no gynecologist is needed, no pranayama, no yoga for pregnancy, and no preparation by the husband. Kunti remained a virgin to the end of her life although she would give birth three more times.

◈

Karna Abandoned

The sun god was still carrying the rakshasa Sahasrabahu in his chariot, where he had hidden after Nara and Narayana had cut off all but two of his thousand arms. When he was invoked by Kunti, Surya thought, "This is a good time to get rid of the guy. Let me shift him from the safe corners back to Earth and let him be killed by Nara and Narayana." So from the region of the sun, Sahasrabahu was sent to Earth to be born as Karna, the first son of Kunti. There was no escape anymore for him.

The baby was beautiful with his shining armor and earrings, but Kunti did not want him and she could not take care of a baby. She was in trouble. It was shameful for an unmarried woman to have a child. It was impossible for her to take it home. So she found a basket, put some nice cushions in it, and placed the child safely on top. She floated the basket into the river, thinking, "I am finished with mantra reciting. I will never chant this mantra again and never invoke any god again; it only creates problems."

The basket drifted on the water and it reached the riverbank near Hastinapura. A man called Adhiratha who was in charge of the king's horses and chariots was roaming around. He saw the basket floating and thought there might be something nice in it, so he went into the water and took it. When he opened it, to his surprise he found a beautiful baby. He brought it home to his wife Radha. They were happy because they had no children of their own, and now at last they had a child to love and take care of. From that time the charioteer and his wife took care of Karna and the child grew up under their care, unaware of his real parents and his lineage.

Although Karna was raised in a humble family he had the genes and the blood of a warrior. He was born from the sun god, and from a member of Krishna's royal family, so he was half divine, half royal. He had his natural protection and he was powerful. When he became eight years old he only liked to play with bow and arrow and nothing else. He achieved unparalleled skills in archery, sword fighting, and all kinds of martial arts. He could contact

Surya. When he stood out in the sun and prayed to Surya, the divine power came out of the sun disk to talk with him and help him.

But when he came to know that he was not the son of the charioteer, he used to wonder and be angry toward his mother who had floated him in the river so that he could never know her. It was a great wound that could not be healed; he suffered from it his entire life. More difficulties in his life were caused by being considered the son of a charioteer, a job with the status of a servant. It would make him feel inferior.

———◆———

Karna was dissatisfied throughout his life because he had been abandoned by his own mother. Kunti not facing the truth was a terrible misfortune for Karna.

10

Birth of the Kauravas and Pandavas

Meanwhile at the royal court of Hastinapura things were going well and the three sons of Vyasa—Dhritarashtra, Pandu, and Vidura—were growing up. They were treated as brothers even though Vidura was the son of a maidservant. To give them a proper education Bhishma sent them to the ashram of Kripa, the family teacher, and Kripa's foster father, the great rishi Gautama. The three boys learned the scriptures and the martial arts that were necessary for *kshatriyas* (warriors). Vidura's main subject was philosophy and he also learned martial arts, but he never used them. He was close with Dhritarashtra and took care of him as a servant. Vidura helped Dhritarashtra to understand things like grammar. Although Dhritarashtra was blind he learned martial arts by working with sound, and he became a master at fighting with spears.

Pandu Becomes King

According to the law the eldest in the family should become king, but when Dhritarashtra was going to be crowned, Vidura, the law giver and prime minister, stood up and said that according to the ancient scriptures a king should not be disabled because he would not be able to save his subjects. Bhishma also pleaded in the name of the scriptures and people accepted what he and Vidura said because they had a lot of authority.

In fact, Bhishma and Vidura's judgment was against the law and against human psychology; when you blindly adhere to what is written in scriptures then you can make such mistakes. The family should have avoided problems by making Dhritarashtra king and letting Pandu manage the affairs of the state as a representative of the king. That way both Dhritarashtra and Pandu would have gotten their due. Instead the kingdom was given to Pandu, who was well built and nice looking. That caused big problems.

As Dhritarashtra had grown up as the eldest prince, expecting to become king, it hurt him badly when Pandu was made king. He felt that god had been unjust to him. When his mother Ambalika had stood in front of Vyasa she had closed her eyes and therefore he had been born blind, so the fault was with her. Or maybe the fault had been with his grandmother Satyavati, who had been impatient to get a legal heir. But surely he had not deserved to be born blind. God had been unjust by making him blind and people had been unjust to him by crowning Pandu instead of him.

———◆———

Dhritarashtra resented that he had been treated like that and he suffered from an inferiority complex. He very much wanted power over the kingdom. He was craving to be king. When you are attached to something you become blind to its bad sides. Like Dhritarashtra we all feel we are disabled and we do not get what we want. People who don't get up in the morning are disabled and they can't do anything during the day. Disabled people are denied the kingdom.

❦

Birth of the Kauravas

Bhishma was powerful and because of his power madness he attacked the king of Gandhara to force him to marry his daughter, princess Gandhari, to Dhritarashtra. He threatened to fight him if he refused the proposal. Since nobody in the kingdom was a match for Bhishma, a fight would have meant the destruction of Gandhara, so the king was compelled to accept the proposal. Otherwise no king would have married his daughter to a blind man. Everybody resented the idea of marrying a beautiful lady to a blind man even if he was royalty. Gandhari's brother prince Shakuni especially opposed it. He felt it was a big insult to him that Bhishma forced his father to accept the preposterous proposal. He swore to take revenge on Bhishma and to destroy his whole clan and the kingdom of Hastinapura. By deception and intrigue he would try to reach his aim.

Bhishma brought lady Gandhari to Hastinapura where she married Dhritarashtra. She understood that if she lived with her husband and talked all the time about things she saw, she would constantly confront her husband with his blindness and cause marriage problems. She decided to blindly follow her husband and save her marriage by tying a cloth over her eyes. Because she had the strength to renounce the pleasure of sight and follow her husband, she was considered a high lady. She always spoke wisely. However, covering her eyes became irresponsible when they had children.

Gandhari got pregnant and she remained pregnant for two years, but no child was born. She asked for her belly to be struck and then a hard ball of flesh came out of her body. Vyasa was consulted and, following his instructions, the ball was divided into a hundred parts that were kept in a hundred pots and allowed to grow. From the hundred pots came ninety-nine boys and one girl (Duhsala).

Duryodhana was the eldest and the main son. Of all their children the king and his wife loved Duryodhana the most. But he was the most malicious one. He always talked bad and he always wanted to put salt on wounds to make them burn more. Even with his uncle Vidura and grandfather Bhishma he *behaved arrogantly. Gandhari and Dhritarashtra's second son was Dushasana. He was full of aggression and blindly followed Duryodhana.*

Duryodhana had all the qualities of ego (*ahamkara*) and he did not find a solution to get away from his ego problems. This was because he did not find the kingdom that he desired most. Fathers and mothers need to spend time together with their children. When both the father and the mother do not look after their children and leave them to babysitters then the children become spoiled.

Discontentment

Many times the *gopis* (female cowherds) in Vrindavan held the little boy Krishna by his ear and brought him to his mother because he was stealing butter. His mother used to ask why he stole butter when they had so much in the house. They were rich people with thousands of cows and lots of milk and butter. A child who has so much butter at home should not steal butter. But the butter at home is not as good as the butter in somebody else's pot. Similarly the money in your own pocket doesn't look like much, but in somebody else's hand it does. Like that there are many things. Human beings are never content with anything and this discontentment is a big problem.

Birth of the Pandavas

Pandu married twice, each time for political reasons. The marriage with Kunti united Hastinapura with the area near Mathura and Vrindavan. Then Bhishma advised Pandu to unite with the kingdom of Madra, east of the present region of Uttar Pradesh, by marrying Madri, the sister of the king of Madra. Both times, on the first day after the wedding ceremony, King Pandu was informed that enemies were attacking the borders. He immediately had to say goodbye to his newly wedded wife and leave with his army.

Every king had a religious duty to see that the borders of his kingdom were well secured. Instead of "loving his neighbor as himself," a king had to treat his neighbor as an enemy that had to be conquered if possible to expand the country. Then the army of that king was used to strengthen the borders. Pandu was a great warrior. He subdued all the neighboring kings and made the kingdom big and strong, so he was recognized as the great king of Hastinapura.

Finally, after all the fighting, he had some time to relax. He wanted to get away from responsibilities and fighting and go on a retreat in the forest with his two wives. Before he left he handed over the kingdom to Dhritarashtra and asked him to take care of it. Nobody knew that Pandu would never see his kingdom again.

In the forest Pandu was relaxing, meeting rishis, and talking about dharma, and they convinced him to get ready to have children. But during a hunt in the forest he thought he saw a deer and he shot. That was a great mistake. A human cry sounded through the forest. It was from a rishi. He and his wife had been playing as deer to enjoy their animal nature.

When a person is making love the energy goes down to the lower chakras and the person gets into frequencies of animal incarnations. To enjoy their animal frequencies the rishi and his wife had locked their chakras and assumed an animal form in which they could play while keeping their energy in their higher chakras. The most harmless and most beautiful animal is a deer. That's why everybody calls his or her beloved "my dear." So the rishi and his wife were enjoying making love as deer.

When King Pandu shot the fatal arrow, the deer changed form and became human again. The dying rishi spoke, "You have shot us while we were copulating, so we curse you that whenever you try to make love with a woman you will die."

That was too much for Pandu, because he had two wives and he wanted

to have children, but he could not have any or else he would die. He decided
that he should do penance to purify himself from having killed the rishi and
his wife although everybody said that it had been an accident and that he had
not intentionally shot at them. He did not return to his kingdom, but he joined
the group of ascetics living in a nearby ashram in the forest. He renounced the
life of luxury and started wearing the clothes of a hermit.

Again the kingdom of Hastinapura faced the problem of lacking a legal
heir. One day Pandu explained to Kunti that he wanted children, but he
would die if he made love to her. Then Kunti told him she could have children
anyhow because of the mantra she had learned from the great rishi Durvasa
when she was a little girl. Using that mantra she could beget as many sons
as she wanted. Pandu said, "Then please invoke Dharma." So Kunti invoked
Dharma (Dharmaraja or Yama) and got a son whose name was Yudhishthira.
A year later she invoked the god of wind Vayu (or Maruta) and she got a son
who was called Bhima. A few years after that she invoked Indra, the god of
subgods and demigods, and got Arjuna.

Then Pandu asked Kunti to teach the mantra also to Madri so she would
not feel bad about Kunti having three children when she had none. So Kunti
did, and Madri invoked the two Ashwini Kumars, the twins who are great
medicine men and healers, and she got Nakula and Sahadeva, the youngest
of the Pandava brothers. All the babies were born without long pregnancies;
they were right there when the energy was invoked. They grew up in the
forest. They were educated by the rishis in the ashram, and they lived like
brahmacharis. Belonging to the kshatriya caste, they were taught all things
suitable for warriors, but they did not know that they were from the royal
dynasty of Hastinapura.

———◆———

Dhritarashtra Becomes King

One day Pandu became fascinated by his wife Madri bathing in the river. He
became undisciplined (which is a disease of mind) and wanted to make love

with her. He accepted the challenge of the time although he knew it would kill him. He approached her, and the minute he tried to make love to her he died. Madri felt guilty and thought that she was responsible for the death of her husband, thinking that if she had not been bathing in the river, he would still have been alive. At that time it was a tradition that a woman would willfully burn herself on the funeral pyre of her husband. It was a special ritual called sati, which is now illegal. The idea was to avoid being a widow, to again take birth and reunite with her husband. A woman of those times did not consider marrying any other man whereas a modern woman prefers to have a different husband in her next life.

Madri asked Kunti, the first wife of Pandu, "Please take care of your children and mine. I will go with my husband." Kunti agreed because it was in accordance with tradition. Madri handed over her children Nakula and Sahadeva to Kunti and sacrificed her life with the life of her husband. When Madri was gone, Kunti remained in the forest with five children. The rishis helped Kunti to educate them.

Before Pandu had left for the retreat from which he never returned, he had handed over the kingdom to Dhritarashtra and asked him to rule it in his name. So Dhritarashtra was the ruler of the kingdom, but rather than being king, he was just the caretaker. When Pandu died there was nobody else in the family to become king, so Dhritarashtra became king after all. Vidura became a counselor and prime minister to Dhritarashtra. He was frank with the blind king because they had grown up together, but with others he mostly kept silent.

———◆———

Dhritarashtra had the life of a king with servants and prime ministers and he was living in the royal palace, but he had never been officially crowned. If he had been made the king in the very beginning he would not have become resentful. But because he had not been properly prepared for the job of king and he always felt that the kingdom could be taken away any minute, he did not feel responsible for it. It was an ego problem that he did not really feel he was the true king.

☙❦☙

The Pandavas Move to the Palace

The rishis saw that the Pandavas should go back to the palace because otherwise they would lose the kingdom. They counseled Kunti to take the five boys to the royal palace of Hastinapura. Dhritarashtra received them and gave them a place to stay there. They were educated by Kripa, the common teacher (kula guru) of the royal family, who also educated the hundred children of Dhritarashtra. The children of Pandu were called Pandavas and the children of Dhritarashtra were called Kauravas because they came from the family of Kuru.*

The Pandavas had the legal claim on the crown because it had belonged to their father and Duryodhana only had a claim on the crown because his father ruled the country as a regent. Duryodhana and his brothers felt bad about it and started disliking their cousin brothers. Duryodhana would ask his father why the Pandavas were allowed to live in the palace, and his father would answer that family members should be allowed to live in the palace. The situation was unbearable to Duryodhana; slowly he became the enemy of the Pandavas. In the long run it resulted in war as a natural result of the course of events over many years.

Krishna regularly visited the palace because Kunti was his aunt. There he also met her sons, his cousin brothers. Like them, Krishna came from a family of warriors. Yudhishthira and Bhima were older than he, but Arjuna was almost the same age, and they played together a lot. Yudhishthira, being the son of Dharma, was very honest and just. He did not want to do any wrong. He was a gyani (scholar), so he judged everything by knowledge. He always asked himself how things had happened and how they should have happened. He was beyond hatred; if somebody misbehaved because he was not feeling well, then he excused him. He was respectful when necessary and otherwise he was neutral. Bhima had a lot of power. Since power makes people arrogant,

---

Kaurava generally refers to all descendants of Kuru, which included the Pandavas, but in a narrower way it refers to just the descendants of Dhritarashtra because he was eldest of the clan.

Bhima was very arrogant. He was eager to fight because he was mad with power and aggression.

At a young age Arjuna was already brilliant. He was generous, respectful, humble, and loving; he did not do much harm. He was not interested in fighting, wealth, name, kingdom, or revenge. He had studied the scriptures and he had knowledge, but he was more of a bhakta (devotee) than a gyani (scholar). He was a romantic hero, an expert archer who could also sing and dance. People everywhere were attracted to him. His devotion to Krishna was exemplary and Krishna saved him from lots of troubles. His main advantage over everybody else was his humility. Nakula and Sahadeva kept things in their hearts and did not express them.

————◆————

11

Drona, Drupada, and the Legacy of Revenge

The story of the Pandavas and the Kauravas intertwines with that of Drona and Drupada and that of Kunti's first son, Karna. When they were young boys, Drona and Drupada studied together in Drona's father's ashram. Even though Drupada was the son of the king and Drona's father was only a poor teacher, they became friends. Once Drupada told Drona, "When I become the king, I will give you half of my kingdom." It was just silly talk like sometimes people promise a big present "when they win the lottery." In friendship people sometimes say things that they cannot fulfill. At that time Drupada was just a student who did not own anything, and having a kingdom was like winning a lottery for him. Later when he had become king he realized he did not have the right to give half of his kingdom away. Foolishly, Drona took it seriously. He thought that when Drupada became king, he really would get half of the kingdom or at least some wealth. A poor man always thinks about getting rich and for that he trusts his friends because they are his only source. But often rich friends are no help.

Drupada Hurts Drona

Many years later Drona married Kripi, who, along with her brother Kripa had been found as babies abandoned near the Ganges river by King Shantanu. Drona and Kripi had a son whose name was Ashvatthama. One day the child was hungry and crying for milk. Kripi said, "You are a friend of King Drupada. Why don't you go and ask him to give you a job or some money so that we can have a cow and milk for our son?" That compelled Drona to visit Drupada.

When Drona arrived in the palace he greeted Drupada as a friend, but the king did not like a poor brahmin addressing him as a friend without asking permission. He said, "You have no right to call me friend. Kings are friends with kings but not with poor people."

Drona reminded him that they had been classmates and how close their friendship had been and that he had promised him half of the kingdom. The king replied, "Maybe I said something like that, but that does not mean anything." Drona asked at least to be treated well, but Drupada told him to get out of there. Drona had expected so much and then he got treated like that. He was hurt so badly that he could not bear it and decided to take revenge. He waited many years for an opportunity to teach Drupada a lesson.

———◆———

Drona's desire for revenge was a weakness in his character. Most people who have perfected some art develop a kind of pride, and when somebody insults them they feel very insulted and then they want to teach the person a lesson. Apart from that Drona had a good character. He was stable and could not easily be persuaded to move from his path.

◦❧◦

Drona, Teacher of Princes

One day when the Pandava children were playing their ball fell in a well and the children did not know how to take it out. Drona came by and offered help. He picked up straws from nearby and shot them like arrows one after another and they all became one. Then he pulled the straws and the ball came out. Nobody else could have done that. The children ran to Bhishma to tell him that there was an expert in archery around who had helped them to get their ball back. Bhishma found out that Drona was the brother-in-law of Kripa, the teacher of the Pandavas and Kauravas. Like Bhishma, Drona had been a disciple of Parashurama. Bhishma called Drona and asked him to become the teacher of the Pandava and Kaurava children.

From times immemorial tests have been popular at schools. Usually after every month of study there is a test. If you pass it then you are considered a good boy; otherwise you are a bad boy. I don't like it personally, but it helps you to understand your progress. Drona also wanted to test his students.

Drona made a bird of wax and put it on a tree. He made a mark on the ground and then he called his pupils one by one. Yudhishthira had to come first because he was the eldest in the clan. Drona asked, "Yudhishthira, do you see that bird on the tree?"

Yudhishthira said, "Yes, I do."

Drona said, "Aim at the eye of the bird, but before you shoot, tell me what you see."

Yudhishthira said, "I see the eye of the bird, I see the branch on which it is sitting, I see leaves and a little bit of clouds."

Drona said, "Don't shoot. Step back."

And Yudhishthira went back. Then Drona called Bhima, Duryodhana, and the others. He asked everyone the same question, "What do you see?" And they said, "I see the bird, the beak of the bird, the neck, and I see the branch of the tree."

Each time Drona said, "Get away, you can't do it." So everybody failed the test. But then it was Arjuna's turn. Drona said, "Arjuna come here and aim. Now tell me, what do you see?"

Arjuna said, "I only see the eye of the bird."

Drona said, "You shoot!" and Arjuna shot his arrow right in the eye. Drona said, "As long as you see the beak, the head, the feathers, the branch, and all around the bird, you are not able to shoot the eye. You have to learn to see only the eye of the bird. Then you can do everything with full concentration and without effort."

The story shows how much Arjuna concentrated on what he had to do whereas all the others were less pinpointed. As long as you are distracted by side issues, you cannot solve the main problem. Education is mostly about teaching a student how to become pinpointed. There are books and libraries full of knowledge and anybody can be a learned person by studying the books. But why don't people who are going to libraries become great scholars? And why is the librarian who knows all about all books not the biggest scholar? That is because one can only master a subject by devoting his time and energy to it. In India when somebody is distracted a lot then they often say, "Hey, the eye of Arjuna should be only on the eye of the bird and not on other things!" Then the person remembers the story and concentrates more.

Some animals also have a good power of concentration. Predators especially need to be centered for their hunt. They are not like vegetarians who can gather fruits or get hold of a plant and eat it. Hunters work with creatures as clever as they are and their prey runs away to save its life. If a hunter is not centered he doesn't catch anything. So hunters need to have a great concentration. Everybody should practice some hunting (without killing) in life to learn to concentrate.

Drona was a real teacher who taught his students how to save themselves. He was above good and bad guys. He would teach everybody: his students, friends, and even his enemies. Arjuna was his most favorite student, and nobody respected Drona as much as Arjuna. Arjuna had faith in him and so much reverence and respect for him that Drona was his point of reference. When people visited the school and asked the students, "Who are you?" they would say something like, "I am Yudhishthira, son of Pandu of Hastinapura," or "I am Duryodhana, son of Dhritarashtra from Hastinapura," but Arjuna replied, "I am a student of Drona and Arjuna is my name." For Arjuna the name of his teacher was more important than his own name. Devotion to the teacher is called guru bhakti *and the reward of guru bhakti is siddhi (spiritual power). Arjuna could do everything perfectly because he did not put himself forward as important.*

———◆———

⊙Ⱦ⊙

Drona and Ekalavya

Ekalavya wanted to become student of Drona, but he was refused because he was from a low caste. Then the boy made a clay sculpture of Drona and took that as his teacher, and after several years he became an excellent archer. One day he met Arjuna who was impressed by his skill and asked him the name of his teacher. Ekalavya claimed to be a student of Drona. Then Arjuna complained to Drona that he had trained another student who was outstanding. Drona went to Ekalavya and asked his fee (gurudakshina). Drona asked him for his right thumb, which Ekalavya gave without hesitation.

———◆———

The cultural gap between India and the West can make it very difficult to understand this story. Drona was born in a caste system, which may seem wrong to you, but for him it was dharma; demanding the thumb meant following his dharma, but to people from other traditions it appears cruel. At the same time we need to keep in mind that Drona's request made a small character from a low caste immortal. He became so special that still today everybody sympathizes with him. People remember him with more reverence than Arjuna. Otherwise he would just have been one of many experts in archery.

Of course, Drona never thought about Ekalavya becoming immortalized. Most of the time things happen when people don't think about the consequences. Drona wanted to show that a person can become the best in martial arts if he has such devotion to his guru, which Ekalavya showed by offering his thumb at his command. It was a lesson for all the princes who were his students but who would not do that. It added so much glamour to the character of Ekalavya that out of many characters in Mahabharata, his name shines like a star.

When we read that story it impresses us because of Ekalavya's sacrifice and his following of dharma. A person's dharma depends upon the role that he or she is playing. Ekalavya is an example of how a person can be full of respect and love for his teacher, even though Drona had not accepted him as a student. But Ekalavya had accepted Drona as his guru and selected the role of being a disciple of Drona, so to him it was his dharma to obey Drona's command.

The thumb is important in archery, but it is possible to learn to work without it. The story of Ekalavya's life exists. After a few years he had that skill again and later on in Mahabharata and other places he shows that without his thumb he was equally a good warrior and equally a good archer. A little thumb really is not so much.

☙❧

Karna Is Cursed

As a boy Karna used to watch the princes play and learn in Drona's school. One day he asked to be admitted to Drona's school so that he could train in the martial arts. Drona refused him because the school belonged to King Dhritarashtra and only people from the royal family could study in it. That felt like a blow to Karna and it started his jealousy toward Arjuna. As Karna had royal blood, he was ambitious and he wanted to go high in his life. He could not swallow being refused admittance in Drona's ashram for being the son of a charioteer.

Then Karna went to Parashurama, who had been the teacher of Drona and Bhishma. Because kshatriyas had done wrong to the brahmins, Parashurama had taken a vow to eradicate all kshatriyas from the surface of the earth; he also vowed he would teach his knowledge only to brahmins and never to any warrior. Karna deceived Parashurama and pretended to be a brahmin in order to be accepted as his student.

One day, after Karna had studied with Parashurama for some time, Parashurama felt sleepy. He said to Karna, "I am tired and I want to rest. Just wait a few minutes here, then I will be free and we can go on together." Karna supported the head of his guru on his thigh to help him relax. While Parashurama was sleeping a biting spider crawled on Karna's body and bit his thigh. Karna was afraid to awake his guru and without moving he kept on supporting Parashurama's head while he endured the pain. The spider cut deep into Karna's body and some drops of blood fell on Parashurama and woke him up.

When Parashurama saw the blood he thought that most brahmins could not bear such pain. He said, "Tell me, are you a brahmin or a kshatriya?"

Karna did not dare to lie anymore and he said, "Because you teach your science to brahmins only, I pretended to be one but I am not."

Parashurama became angry and said, "You learned my knowledge by deceiving me. I will give you a curse that when you are in the battlefield needing my knowledge the most you will forget it and it will not help you. You can use the divine weapons that I taught you and terrify the whole world, but in the most critical situation of your life you will forget how to use them." This was the first of a set of curses that would pile up in Karna's life as a cloud of doom hanging above his head.

Karna left the ashram and in due time he visited other gurus and acquired more skills. One day he was hunting animals in the forest. Riding his chariot, he chased some animals who had been grazing. Among them was a cow that panicked and ran into a pool of quicksand where she got stuck. While she was drowning she cursed him saying, "You chased me into this mud where I am stuck but before I drown I give you a curse that when you are on the battlefield fighting the most important battle of your life, your chariot will get stuck. Just as I am caught by mud, so your chariot wheel will get stuck in the mud; you will not be able to get it out and then you will be killed." This was the second big curse that Karna received. He received curses the way Arjuna received blessings.

———◆———

◦¥◦

Karna Gains a Friend

Drona's students had finished their education in martial arts. A big perfor-
mance was organized in which the princes had to show their skills. A large
stage was set up where people could assemble. The students were giving
demonstrations of sword fighting, horse riding, and other royal sports. Arjuna
showed his skills in the art of archery. He created a bridge of arrows and he
shot arrows at such speed that they formed an umbrella over his head and not
even a drop of rain could pass through it.

In those days Karna, Arjuna, and Dhrishtadyumna, the commander
in chief of the Pandava army, were the best archers and sword fighters.
Karna had been watching Arjuna and said, "Let me show you that I can
do better than you and I challenge you to do what I can." But Kripa, the
family teacher of the Pandavas and Kauravas, got up and said, "You are
challenging Arjuna, a son of Pandu, the greatest warrior of his time. He is a
distinguished member of the royal family of Hastinapura. Now tell me from
which family do you come?" Karna was confused because he did not know
his lineage. If he said that he was the son of a charioteer he would not be
allowed to challenge Arjuna, and if he didn't tell them he would be refused
as well. This embarrassment increased Karna's hatred toward Arjuna and his
family. Kunti had recognized him from a distance because he was the only
one who was born with earrings of his own flesh. If she had stood up and
said that Karna was her son with the sun god himself then the Mahabharata
story would have been different. But she did not dare to tell because having
a child before being married caused a scandal in those days; even nowadays
some people cannot accept it.

Karna felt bad and he was about to leave when Duryodhana, who was
always against the Pandavas, stepped forward and said, "If belonging to a
royal family is the only criterion to join the competition, I will give him a
royal status. I am the emperor of this part of the country and I give one of
my kingdoms to Karna. So from today onward he is the king of Anga. And as
a king he can challenge a son of a king." Duryodhana called a priest, got the

ritual done, gave Karna a crown, and made him the king of Anga, which was a part of Bihar. But at that time the sun was setting. The day was over and the games were finished. In spite of Duryodhana's efforts Karna did not have an opportunity to defeat Arjuna. But Duryodhana had won Karna's heart by helping him and they became friends. However, Duryodhana's uncle Shakuni did not like Karna because Karna was honest and a follower of dharma.

———◆———

Drona's Revenge

It was a tradition that at the end of their education students would ask their teacher what fee (gurudakshina) he would like. So his students came to Drona with sweets and flowers and asked, "Sir, please tell us what do we have to give you as a fee for our education?" Drona said, "I want you to arrest King Drupada and bring him in front of me because he has treated me badly. He is proud that he is a king and that he has studied the art of fighting and archery from my father and other great teachers. Nobody can bind him. Tie his hands and feet and bring him here in a rude manner so that he realizes that power is not the only thing."

Duryodhana and his brothers said, "We should get the chance first." Drona gave in. They all went, but Drupada disturbed their army, defeated them, and they all had to run away. Then they came back to Drona and admitted that they could not do it.

Then Drona said to Arjuna, "You are my favorite disciple, now you go and do it." Arjuna went there and he fought Drupada, arrested him, and brought him before Drona. It was very humiliating for Drupada. Drona said, "As you said, a king is only a friend of kings. I cannot call you my friend, though in my heart I still feel friendship for you. I brought you here in this condition because you were too proud of your power and I wanted to break your ego. I trained my students to show you that they have more power than you. Now you are in my hands and I can punish you any way I like. But my punishment is that you should feel sorry about your misbehavior. By being defeated your kingdom became mine because whenever a king is defeated his kingdom belongs to the winner. But I don't need your kingdom and I give it back to you; this humiliation is enough."

Drupada felt sad, but instead of changing his life and becoming a better person, he held a grudge against Drona. The only aim in his life became to somehow defeat Drona, to get him killed or destroy his power. With that in his mind he worshipped and performed an important yagya.* Drupada did the yagya to take revenge on Drona. From the fire a son was born whose name was Dhrishtadyumna. Later he would be the one who would stab a sword through Drona's body. From the same fire a girl was also born whose name was Draupadi. She was pure, strong, intelligent, and beautiful. Because of her dark complexion she also was called Krishna. She grew up in the palace of her father. It was predicted that Draupadi would be the cause of a war that would destroy the Kauravas.

———◆———

---

*A yagya, or homa, is a fire worship in which mantras are recited and herbs, ghee, and other things are offered to the fire. In the end when the yagya is complete, whatever you want as the fruit of your karma comes to you.

12
How the Pandavas Got Married

Mistakes always become problems. It was a mistake that at first the kingdom was given to Pandu instead of Dhritarashtra. That grew into a problem. Dhritarashtra's sons were born with all his unfulfilled desires. This happens so often. I know lots of people who try to make their children what they could not become. When Duryodhana grew up Dhritarashtra inspired him to become king, but it was against the law of dharma because the kingdom had legally been given to his brother Pandu. When Pandu went to the forest for a retreat he had said, "I am giving you my crown. Wear it and rule the kingdom in my name." He did not say, "Now you are the king forever and you can do as you like." He said, "Rule the kingdom in my name." That meant that the crown still belonged to Pandu and that his sons were the legal heirs.

Dhritarashtra put the seed of his inferiority complex in Duryodhana. Many times he told him, "You are living in the palace, you are the prince, but one day your nephews will claim the kingdom. Their father became king only because he was not disabled like me. Although they don't have the right they will try to take away the kingdom from you." That way Dhritarashtra himself created enmity toward the Pandavas. There was a kind of inner war between the Pandavas and the Kauravas, but the hundred Kauravas never won over the five Pandavas. Several times Duryodhana tried to kill one or all of the Pandavas. The first time was when they were students.

☙✦❧

The Kauravas Poison Bhima

Bhima was a son of the wind god Vayu. Power goes with the vayu element (air) and all jobs requiring power are done by vayu. So Bhima was exceptionally strong. But Bhima had problems controlling his power. He used to talk bluntly without regard to whom he was talking. He always liked to display his strength as power generally does. He uprooted trees and lifted big stones. He sat down in the river and stopped all the water.

Bhima always created problems for the Kaurava brothers. When they had climbed a tree to pick mangos he would shake the tree so that they all fell down like fruits. Sometimes he would take ten of them on one side and ten on the other and drag their heads against each other; that was really awful. The display of so much power made Duryodhana and his brothers jealous and afraid. Their fear made them aggressive toward the Pandavas and toward Bhima in particular. They wanted to destroy him, but that just made him more arrogant.

Duryodhana knew that Bhima was a ferocious eater. He could eat hundreds of sweet balls and he was fond of sweet milk pudding (kheer). So Duryodhana and Dushsasana made a lot of kheer and put poison in it. They expected that Bhima would see it and eat it all just to tease them. Killing Bhima would solve their biggest worry because the other four brothers were much easier to get rid of and Duryodhana could take care of them. Their plan worked. When Bhima saw the kheer he finished it all before anybody else could claim his share. He fell unconscious. The Kaurava brothers picked up his body, took it to the river, and threw it in so that it would be carried away by the current and would not be found. Then they started relaxing, pretending that nothing had happened.

By the evening when Bhima had not shown up his brothers got worried.

They searched all around within an area of several miles, but they did not find him. They were sad and started thinking something had happened to him. Meanwhile Bhima was drifting in the water. He floated down the river, into the ocean, and from there into the underworld (patala loka). In the underworld are only snakes (nagas) who live under water and demons or rakshasas who eat meat, drink liquor, and dance in the disco. Any human was considered an intruder. The snakes bit Bhima, but their poison neutralized Duryodhana's poison and he came back to life.* The snakes got hold of Bhima and brought him to their king. By chance one of the snakes, Aryaka, was a great grandfather of Kunti, so when Bhima had introduced himself Aryaka said, "Welcome to the underworld. I am the grandfather of your maternal grandfather, so we are family. What happened, how did you get here?"

Bhima said, "I don't know, I was at home eating a sweet dish and then I fell unconscious. When I came to my senses I saw all these snakes around me and they took hold of me. That's all I know."

The king said, "You were poisoned, but the poison was cured by snake bites. I will give you an elixir to make your body invincible. No weapon will be able to harm you, no poison will be able to kill you, so you will be almost immortal."

If Bhima had not been poisoned he would never have gotten that elixir. And then he returned home even more powerful. So instead of killing him the Kauravas had made him stronger. He was not afraid of anything because nothing could wound him anymore. Duryodhana tried other ways of eliminating Bhima, but he never succeeded. Bhima was strong and a good fighter with a club, and nobody ever defeated him.

The Negative Side of Support

During the first two yugas, Satya Yuga and Treta Yuga, people lived in ashrams. They were free to come and go whenever they wanted and

---

*If you give a poisoned man an injection of cobra venom then poison cures poison.

they did not form fixed groups. If something wrong happened, then all people felt free to go to the king and protest. In Dvapara Yuga the king gradually became isolated from the people and he became a point of fear and terror. The more architecture improved, the higher the walls that surrounded the palace. That created problems; at the end of Dvapara Yuga the common people did not participate or protest anymore, they just let warriors, courtiers, and ministers take care of affairs. Fixed groups came into being.

Duryodhana organized a group of people who supported him and agreed with him, whether he was right or wrong. His brothers were organized like an army and Duryodhana was the commander in chief. So as a child he already had an army of his own to support him, but that kind of support creates problems. Nowadays we also build walls to isolate ourselves from people who clearly tell us our weak points and we also collect people around us who blindly support us. In psychological language these walls and support groups represent ego problems and in metaphysical language they are ignorance, blindness, and not understanding the truth.

After her marriage Gandhari called her brother Shakuni to come and help, so he came and lived at the court. The relationship between him and King Dhritarashtra was delicate. If you want to be at peace with your wife, you should be nice to her brother. Shakuni took advantage of that to create enmity between the Pandavas and the Kauravas, hoping that they would fight and kill each other. Because he was tortured by anger it was his purpose to take revenge on Bhishma and his clan and destroy them all. It would be sad for his sister, but he was completely taken over by his desire for revenge. He was a deceitful man who used his position to attain his end. By spoiling Duryodhana he was able to cause the destruction of the Kaurava dynasty. Many times Gandhari told him to stop interfering with the affairs of the Pandavas and Kauravas and go back home. He always replied that he could not go because his job was not yet done.

Dhritarashtra lacked the courage to stop Duryodhana from doing wrong things. That lack of courage was because he had surrendered to his desire to be important and his desire to be king. Duryodhana could do whatever he liked without his parents controlling him. Dhritarashtra was blind and his wife had blindfolded herself and they just let everything happen. Both parents were neglecting their children, so Duryodhana could associate with Shakuni, Karna, and Ashvatthama, who all used to help him do wrong things. If mother and father would have paid more attention to their children then maybe they could have taken Duryodhana out of that bad company or at least have had some positive effect on him and he would have become less evil. But they were modern people with babysitters and they had no time to sit with their babies themselves.

Kingdom and territorial complex are attributes of third-chakra energy, which creates many problems. The kingdom may be big or small, but the feeling is the same: "I won't allow anybody to intrude in my kingdom." If self-glorification arising from the second chakra becomes instrumental in this, then the problems become more severe, and that's what happened.

The House of Lacquer

Because of jealousy and greed Duryodhana did not want to share the kingdom with the Pandavas; he wanted it all for himself. After the attempt to kill Bhima by poison, he planned another attack to finally get rid of them all. He conspired with his friend Karna and his uncle Shakuni, who advised him to build a house of lacquer. They hired good architects to design it and skilled laborers to build it. It was beautiful, but it was made of highly inflammable materials like bamboo, fat, hair, dry leaves, and lacquer.* They knew a small flame would be enough to set it on fire. When it was finished they called the

---

*In India a type of resin or lacquer is obtained from banyans and other trees. It is like a parasite that appears on the branches and eats the tree. It is used as varnish and for polishing, and it burns very quickly.

local ruler and told him, "We will send five brothers and their mother to that house. When the time is right and they are at home, you must set the house on fire and let them burn alive."

Duryodhana said to his father, "The Pandavas used to live in an ashram in the forest. They have been living in the palace for a long time without any outing. After finishing their education, why should they unnecessarily stay here? They should have a retreat to enjoy nature for some time. Why not ask them to go and see a part of the kingdom they have never seen?" Dhritarashtra of course gave permission.

Similarly he told mother Kunti, "Since you came to the palace the children have been so busy with their education that they have had no time for an outing or even a picnic. Now you should have a holiday. We have made a nice place for your retreat; you can go and rest there. The local ruler will take care of you and he will arrange everything for you in a royal manner."

The Pandavas were unsuspecting and thought, "Sometimes our brother is good and now he wants us to enjoy, so he arranged everything." They gladly accepted the offer.

But when Vidura was told about Duryodhana's offer, he was suspicious. He soon found out that the house that had been built for the Pandavas consisted of flammable materials. He always protected the good people, but he was a prime minister of the evil, so he could not act openly. When the Pandavas were taking leave of everybody, he warned Yudhishthira saying, "One should not trust somebody who becomes kind without any reason. There must be a reason for Duryodhana suddenly being nice. The house where you are going to live is specially prepared for you. Fire can be anywhere and one should always take care not to get burnt. When a fire comes in the forest the rat always gets saved because he digs a tunnel." So in a concealed way he warned Yudhishthira and his brothers about a fire in the house where they were going to stay and that they should dig a tunnel to escape from it.

Soon after the Pandavas had arrived in the house, a man came. When he saw that nobody else was around he spoke to them. "I have been sent by Vidura. I am an expert in digging tunnels. This house is a deathtrap. Duryodhana wants to set it on fire and burn you all alive. But I will help you to make a tunnel through which you can escape from here before the fire starts. We have to do this work secretly because if somebody from the palace finds out what we are doing then the king will not spare us." Yudhishthira and Bhima promised to keep it a secret, and at night while everybody was asleep the man was digging and Bhima carried all the earth and threw it into the river. In a few nights the man dug a tunnel connecting their bedroom with a village across the river. That way they could get out, and nobody would know where they were.

Duryodhana's plan was that on the full moon night there would be a big feast around the house, and later when people were sleeping the house would be set on fire. By chance a tribal lady who was living nearby came with her five sons. During the feast they had too much liquor and they could not go home. The lady asked Kunti if she could stay for the night. Kunti consented and at night when they were sleeping the Pandavas quietly left the house. When all was quiet and dark the caretaker of the house thought that Kunti and her five sons were sleeping inside and he set the house on fire. The next day six dead bodies were recovered, and it was believed that the Pandava brothers and their mother were dead.* Duryodhana was convinced that his plan had worked and that he had gotten rid of the Pandavas. He was happy and made a big feast. Everybody else was mourning the death of the five princes who were the legal heirs of the kingdom. At the palace the flag of the kingdom was brought down and there was a royal mourning.

———◆———

Leela and Evil

Ego is the sense of being, the isness, I, me, mine. Ego is a false sense of identification that develops because the cosmic consciousness has manifested as the consciousness of many individuals for the sake of *leela* (divine play), to play hide and seek with itself. Without leela everything would stay the same and nothing would happen.

---

*Another version of the story says that Kunti and her sons went through the tunnel and Bhima came back to set the house on fire and that the caretaker who was sleeping at that time also got burnt.

We would always remain cosmic consciousness and we would not be here. The purpose of the game is to steal the butter, to get more cream, and to play with the gopis, the ladies who are fascinations. That is *prakriti* (nature, energy, Shakti), who always wants to be with the *purusha* (cosmic consciousness, supreme being, Shiva).

Life on Earth is a play and we are an essential part of it. Without evil, our life on Earth would be impossible. If we treat evil as the evil, as Christianity has done with the devil, it will create problems. Evil is only that which is not according to the law of dharma at that particular time and place. So evil depends on time, place, moment, and event.

☙❦❧

Ghatotkacha, Son of Bhima

When Kunti and her five sons had escaped through the tunnel they were moving around and then they met another messenger from Vidura saying, "Everybody thinks that you are dead. Please, for your own safety, remain undercover so that nobody knows that you are alive. Change your names, your dress, your way of living, and live somewhere near the forest. Don't go to Hastinapura." They disguised themselves as brahmins and started moving from town to town, never staying in a place for more than a few days.

At one place Bhima met a rakshasa whose name was Hidimba. He was from a man-eating tribe. When he saw the five brothers he became happy that after a long time five humans were around and he could have a feast in the coming night. He asked his sister Hidimbi to keep them busy so that he could come later and grab them. Those rakshasas had the power to change their appearance at will and Hidimbi transformed herself into a beautiful lady. She talked in a beautiful way with Bhima and she fell in love with him. He was the only man befitting her because he was big and strong like the members of her family. She warned him, "Run away from here; my brother is a man-eater and he will come to eat you all."

Bhima put his mother and his brothers in a safe place and asked Hidimbi to take care of them. Then he challenged the rakshasa Hidimba and he managed to kill him. After that he asked his mother and brothers to leave the place and move further. But then Hidimbi asked, "Why are you leaving me alone? I love you."

Bhima answered, "I don't know. We just met a few hours ago and we talked a little, but that does not mean that I love you or that I will take you with me."

She said, "You killed my brother who was the only man who protected me. Now there is no man except you to save and protect me, but you are running away."

Kunti had started liking the lady when she was taking care of them. She told Bhima not to disappoint her and to marry her. So Bhima married the rakshasa lady Hidimbi and a rakshasa son named Ghatotkacha was born. But Bhima did not stay to live with Hidimbi. She told him that if he needed her he could remember her and then she would immediately come but it never happened. Bhima was not very interested in women. He was a wrestler and a bodybuilder who cared more for his own body than for anybody else.

Bhima Kills Bakasu

The Pandavas came to a town near the kingdom of Panchala where King Drupada was ruling. They started living with a brahmin family. The brahmin and his wife were kind and helped them a lot. One morning Kunti got up early in the morning and heard the lady of the house crying. Kunti asked her why she was crying. The lady told her that in the town there was a rakshasa, a demon called Bakasu, who was a man-eater. Previously he had come every day into the town and grabbed anybody he liked to eat. So the whole town had lived in panic all the time. The king was not powerful enough to defeat the demon, so he had made a pact with him to make the kingdom more peaceful. They had agreed that the demon would stay in his cave and not disturb the kingdom by unnecessarily hunting for food. Each day one person would be sent to him as food.

From that time it became a tradition that in turn every house would send somebody as the food for the rakshasa and now it was their turn, but she and her husband, son, and daughter, were not able to decide who should go. The husband said, "Let me go. I have lived my life, I have done everything, so I can die."

The wife said, "I am not so important. I have given birth to two children and taken care of them. But now they are grown up, so I have fulfilled the purpose of my life. There is not much left for me to do, so I can die. You can still marry and have more children."

He said, "No, I cannot do that."

She said, "But if you go then I will become a widow and I cannot live without you." The son said, "Okay, I will go."

But the father argued, "No, you have not seen the world. You have not seen anything in life. I cannot let you go."

The daughter said, "Okay, then let me go so that my brother can enjoy life. I am useless, so I can go."

But then the mother said, "No, without you life for me is useless. I cannot tell my secret things to my son. I need you as my confidant."

And the father said, "But I need the son."

They could not decide who should go and the woman was crying. Kunti said, "Wait a minute, let me ask my son who is very strong. He can go and fight the demon."

The brahmin said, "No, you are my guests, and I cannot send a guest to the mouth of a ferocious demon."

But Kunti reassured him, "My son has already defeated many demons and he killed them all so this is nothing new for him. He can take care of it; he will go."

The brahmin and the lady said, "Okay, if you are so kind then we agree."

At the appointed time the king's bullock cart came with big barrels of liquor and beer, meat, fruits, and other food. The man who was being sacrificed would be the driver of the cart. Apart from the wooden cart the demon would devour everything: the drinks, the foods, the two bulls, and the driver.

Bhima went with the cart, and when he had arrived at the demon's cave he said to himself, "Before the demon comes and eats all these nice things, let me first finish them and then I will see if I will fight." So he started eating.

The demon was hungry, and while Bhima was eating the smell of food reached the cave. The demon said, "Oh, somebody has brought the food." When he came out of the cave and saw Bhima he got angry. He said, "Hey, why are you eating my food?"

Bhima said, "I am not eating your food. I am eating my food. Your food is these bullocks. You eat that."

The demon said, "No, I will eat you first. You are big. Today I get food with a fight."

Bhima said, "Okay, then let's do it." Bhima had the boon that nothing could harm him and nobody could defeat him, so he was strong enough to resist the demon's attack. Then he picked up the demon, lifted him in the air, and threw him down on the ground. That broke all of the demon's bones and he died.

When Bhima came back with the remaining food and the bullock cart, it was good news for the town. They no longer had to worry who would be the next victim. They were liberated from that fear forever and everybody was happy.

———◆———

❧

Arjuna Wins Draupadi

The news went around that somebody had killed the demon Bakasu. Duryodhana and Karna said, "Nobody could do that except Bhima. It means that the Pandavas are still alive." But they didn't know where they were or how to get them.

When Drupada, the king of Panchala, heard the news, he also suspected that the Pandavas were still alive. He wanted to marry his daughter Draupadi to Arjuna in order to bring about the destruction of his enemy Drona.

Although Arjuna revered Drona more than god, he would later become an instrument in his death. King Drupada organized a svayamvara for his daughter Draupadi. This svayamvara was special because there was a test of skill and the girl would marry the one who passed the test. Drupada made the test so difficult that only Arjuna and nobody else would be able to pass it. He invited the kings of all neighboring countries to the capital of the Panchala kingdom to take part in the ceremony.

The news of the svayamvara soon reached the village where the Pandavas were living undercover. The capital of Panchala was nearby and out of curiosity many brahmins wanted to attend the svayamvara. The Pandava brothers wanted to join the group of brahmins from the village and asked mother Kunti for her permission. She consented, but she told them to stay with the brahmins and not to reveal their identity. So the Pandava brothers, dressed as brahmins, went to see the svayamvara.

At the capital of Panchala the stage had been set for the marriage. Many kings and princes from nearby countries were there, including Krishna, Duryodhana, and Karna. In the marriage hall a big pot had been filled with oil and a fire under the pot kept it boiling. In the center of the pot was a pole with a rotating wheel on top. A fish had been attached to the wheel and the aspirant husband had to look into the boiling oil and shoot his arrow in the eye of the fish. Draupadi would marry whosoever shot the eye of the fish. But the boiling oil distorted the image and made it difficult to see the reflection of the fish, and because the wheel was rotating it was almost impossible to hit the target.

One by one many tried their luck, but they all missed. Even Karna, who was a great archer, also missed. Drupada started feeling sad, thinking that his daughter was to remain unmarried. Once the condition had been announced it could not be relaxed just to get somebody to marry his daughter. But then a brahmin boy got up from his seat and asked permission for an attempt. The warriors and kings resented the idea of a brahmin participating in the competition. But the brahmins argued that there was no reason why a brahmin should not be allowed to try. So the boy was given permission to try his luck and he succeeded. The brahmins liked a brahmin boy to marry a kshatriya girl, but the kshatriyas got angry about it and they started challenging Arjuna for a fight. When Duryodhana and Karna saw the brahmin boy they understood that it had to be Arjuna, but they had no proof.

In the confusion the brothers left with their prize and they went home to mother Kunti. It all happened just by the way. They had visited the svayamvara as spectators without any plan to try and marry that girl, so they did not think about marriage when they came home with their prize. Kunti was doing some puja in the meditation chamber. The boys said, "Mother, see what we have brought for you." She said, "I am busy, so you better distribute it among yourself."

The brothers and the lady were in trouble because she was not a commodity and how can you distribute one lady between five men? When Kunti had finished her puja and saw the lady she felt sad for what she had said and asked what had happened. They told her the story and said, "What you have said is bad."

Kunti said, "Okay, then change it in the way you want it. Because Arjuna shot the arrow and won the competition, he should marry her."

But then Draupadi said, "No, let it be true the way you said it. I accept what has come to me so let it happen."

Arjuna agreed, "She can be a wife of all five of us but only one by one. In turn she will spend one month with each of us. When she is with one person the others will not think about her. We will make a calendar to note when she will be whose wife. That way we will remain in good shape."

This shows that Draupadi was not troubled by having relationships with five men and that the brothers were not jealous. In real life this would be difficult, but in the story it is simple. It was just one of many violations of the law of dharma at the end of Dvapara Yuga.

Krishna went to Drupada to inform him that the Pandavas were alive and that the brahmin who had won his daughter was Arjuna. Drupada sent an invitation to Draupadi and the Pandavas to come to his palace, and when they arrived he finally recognized Arjuna. But when he heard that his daughter had married not only Arjuna but his brothers as well, he felt bad. Only when she explained him how it had happened and that she had consented to it did he relax.

By now it was widely known that the Pandavas were still alive. Dhritarashtra consulted Bhishma and Vidura, the prime minister, to decide how to react to the new situation. They said diplomatically, "By marrying the daughter of King Drupada, the Pandavas have strengthened our country considerably. A potential threat has become an ally so we should be happy and celebrate. It would be good to become friends with them to strengthen the kingdom of Hastinapura. They should be invited back to the kingdom and they should get a part of the kingdom."

Duryodhana was not in the mood to celebrate. He felt guilty that he had tried to kill his own cousins. To the outside world he was keeping up appearances; only to his inner circle could he show his frustration. Reluctantly he agreed to invite the Pandavas to the palace.

———◆———

Sometimes when we try to harm something it becomes stronger. I remember we sprayed DDT to kill mosquitoes. We thought we had solved the problem, but after some time the mosquitoes became immune to DDT and they were stronger. Gentle methods, on the other hand, can be more successful than energetic methods.

❦

Once Vayu, the wind god, and Surya, the sun god, were talking together and both claimed to be the strongest. They decided to put it to a test. When they saw a man walking on the road with a blanket Vayu said, "The one who can get the blanket off that man is the strongest."

Surya said, "Okay, try."

Vayu blew hard to blow off the blanket but the man wrapped himself in it more and more until Vayu became exhausted and gave up. Then Surya said, "Okay, now see." He became a little more bright, so that the man started feeling hot and took off the blanket. Then Surya became even hotter and the man threw the blanket away because he could not bear it anymore. Vayu wanted to take the blanket by force, ego, but Surya generated more power in himself and then the man gave up.

Instead of creating more power in himself, Duryodhana fought against the Pandavas with force. Several times he tried to kill them, but his jealousy could not destroy the seed of truth in them. He poisoned Bhima, but Bhima survived it and even became stronger. The conspiracy to kill the Pandavas in the house of lacquer also did not work because it resulted in the Pandavas becoming allies with the powerful King Drupada. So Duryodhana's attacks were counterproductive; they increased the hatred in the mind of Bhima and the panic in the mind of Duryodhana, and each time the Pandavas came out stronger.

———◆———

13

Yudhishthira Gambles and Loses Everything

The Pandavas returned to the royal palace of Hastinapura with their bride and started living there again. As their father Pandu had been the crowned king of Hastinapura they had the right to inherit a part of the kingdom. Dhritarashtra decided to give them a piece of land where they would have their own kingdom.

୭୯

Building Indraprastha

Duryodhana said to his father, "The presence of the Pandavas bothers me. People appreciate them more than us. Why don't you give them that barren piece of land where our ancestors started the kingdom of Bharata?* It has become obsolete and useless. They should go there, rebuild it, and restore the glory of our ancestors. They are studious and they can do it. That way they

---

*Duryodhana was referring to the forest of Khandava in the southwest, where the capital of Hastinapura had been long before. The kings from the old Ikshvaku dynasty had ruled the area, but it had been abandoned and only ruins remained of the old palace. Some ruins still exist west of the Yamuna River close to the capital, New Delhi. In more modern times people used to take stones and things from there to use in their houses or to sell to museums, but now the site is protected.

will be out of our palace, busy for years with constructing the place, and we will be free to rule the country in our own way."

Dhritarashtra was attached to Duryodhana and he had no control over him. He could not ask him to accept that the Pandavas surpassed him, so he gave in to the whims of his son. He called Yudhishthira and said, "You know we come from the Ikshvaku dynasty and our old place was in the Khandava forest. Because I am blind I could not go there, but I want you to reestablish the place of our ancestors and make your kingdom there."

Bhima grumbled, "The intention is not good. That place is a ruin and completely barren. If we want to make a place there we will have to bring everything."

But Yudhishthira said, "We can design and construct everything fresh. Here everything is already done, so we have no chance to improve." It was true that they were being cheated, but Yudhishthira accepted the offer. He asked Vishvakarma, the divine architect, to construct a palace, but Vishvakarma said he could not do it. Instead, he recommended an architect called Mayadhanava of "Maya Construction Unlimited" from the Mayan civilization in South America. Yudhishthira called him and he designed an amazing palace, town hall, assembly place, and recreation hall. The barren piece of land that had been of no use became a town where the Pandavas started living. They named it Indraprastha, "the dwelling place of Indra, the lord of the heaven." It was truly a royal monument.

Arjuna and Subhadra

Arjuna liked Subhadra, the younger sister of Krishna, but Balarama, their eldest brother and the head of the family, was guarding her and wanted her to marry a powerful king and become a queen. Balarama had taught Duryodhana how to fight with clubs and he favored Duryodhana to marry Subhadra, but she did not like him. She secretly loved Arjuna whom she had seen many times with Krishna. He was good looking and for her he was the most beautiful man,

but even if he had been less handsome she would have loved him. Krishna
helped Arjuna to marry Subhadra. Most of the time they lived in Indraprastha.
They had a son called Abhimanyu who became a student of Krishna.

The Ascent of the Pandavas

In the Mahabharata the god of dharma (spiritual law, inherent nature,
purpose, duty) is present as Bhishma, Vidura, and Yudhishthira.
Yudhishthira was called Dharmaraja (king of dharma) just like his
father Yama, the lord of death. Because of his honesty, righteousness,
knowledge, and intelligence he was famous and much appreciated by
his people; they asked him to become emperor (king of kings). The
custom was that a king who wanted to become emperor performed
a special sacrifice, the *rajasuya yagya,* in which a horse was allowed
to wander freely while a group of warriors followed it. When the
horse came to the lands of a king who opposed the supremacy of the
emperor-to-be, he had to fight with the warriors. If he lost he had to
accept the supremacy of his opponent, but he was allowed to stay on
his throne.

☙❦❧

Yudhishthira Becomes Emperor

The people said to Yudhishthira, "You have four strong brothers and a good
army, so you can defeat any king who opposes you. You can subdue all nearby
nations and become emperor."

Yudhishthira agreed and asked, "Who might oppose me?" Krishna said,
"Duryodhana and his brothers will not oppose you because you are a part
of them. Actually the kingdom of Hastinapura is ruled from two places by
two allied kings. If you become emperor they also become emperors. Your
biggest opponent is Jarasandha, king of Magadha. He has defeated several
neighboring kings and imprisoned them all. If you defeat him, release the kings
from prison, and allow them to return to their kingdom, they will surely accept

your supremacy. By defeating Jarasandha you will win the support of a whole group of kings and it will be easy to become emperor."

So it was done. It was announced that Yudhishthira would perform the rajasuya yagya in order to be proclaimed emperor of north India. Many kings accepted Yudhishthira's supremacy because he was honest and just. Krishna, Bhima, and Arjuna battled with Jarasandha and defeated him. The kings who were released from Jarasandha's prison were grateful and gladly accepted Yudhishthira as their emperor. Yudhishthira's brothers went all around to conquer the few kings who opposed.

For the inauguration ceremony Yudhishthira invited all the kings from the neighboring countries including Duryodhana and his brothers, Shakuni, Karna, and many others. They came to the palace and took part in the ceremony. Brahmins chanted mantras, Yudhishthira made a big performance, and nice things happened. Everybody was happy except Sishupala, who became enraged and started insulting Lord Krishna. After a hundred insults Krishna released his disc weapon (sudarshan chakra) and slit Sishupala's head. Then the inauguration ceremony was performed without any incidents. When it was completed the visitors were invited to view the palace that had regained its ancient glory.

Draupadi's Insult

Duryodhana was burning with jealousy because he had given a barren piece of land to these five idiots and he had not expected that they would be able to build a new palace there. And now there was a new town and Yudhishthira was even declared emperor! In the evening Duryodhana wanted to tour the palace and enjoy its beauty. Yudhishthira suggested he take a guide because there were many places of illusion and he might get into trouble as had already happened to many people. Duryodhana refused, however, and went alone.

When he was walking around he became even more jealous. Somewhere there was a floor that looked like water and nearby there was a pond that looked like a nice floor. At another place there was a wall that looked like a *door, but the actual door looked like a wall. Several times Duryodhana was a victim of the illusions. He avoided the place that appeared to be a wall until he saw people passing through it comfortably. When he wanted to go out of a door to look at the scenery outside for a minute and enjoy nature, he bumped his head because there was no door. When he saw a floor with water he took off his shoes and lifted his trousers to walk through it but there was no water. And when he stepped on something that looked like a solid floor, he fell in water. Duryodhana was very embarrassed.*

Draupadi was standing on the balcony watching Duryodhana's clumsiness. Seeing him falling in the pond made her hilarious. Words came out from her mouth, which she should never have said: "Look what a pity, the son of the blind man also is blind." Duryodhana came out of the pond, collected his company, and returned to the royal palace in Hastinapura. He was so angry that he wanted revenge for his insult at any cost.

After the death of Pandu it was Duryodhana's father, Dhritarashtra, who had taken care of the Pandavas, so the blind man that Draupadi was mocking was her father-in-law. That was too much. It was against the law of dharma for a lady to mock her father-in-law. Talking like that was not popular even in my childhood and six thousand years ago it was a big offense.

People should be conscious that words can hurt more than swords. Draupadi was unaware of the impact of her words. She was thrilled with joy at being the queen of five valiant warriors. She was in her palace and Duryodhana had been acting clumsy. Just for fun she performed a little satire, but the incident so increased the hostility of Duryodhana that it led to war.

Duryodhana Broods on Revenge

Duryodhana was jealous of the splendor of Indraprastha and he was hurt by Draupadi. He wanted revenge, but he did not know how to get it. The

Pandavas were too strong to start a fight with. Something else was needed, but what? His frustrated desire for revenge made him sick. His uncle Shakuni was a shrewd devil. He noticed that Duryodhana was getting pale and he asked him what the matter was. Duryodhana said, "Draupadi has insulted me so badly that it makes me sick. She should be taught respect for me so that she never ever will insult me again."

Everybody likes to invite people to do what they are doing: a shrewd person will advise everybody to become shrewd, a vegetarian will ask everybody to become a vegetarian, and a person going to a beer garden will invite everybody to have a drink.

Shakuni said, "The problem is that the Pandavas are too strong to fight. If you want revenge you better act shrewdly. Even though the great Yudhishthira is the son of Dharma, he has a weakness. He likes to play dice although he plays like an absolute beginner. On the day of his inauguration ceremony we played dice and I let him win only to lure him, but I could have easily won because I am an expert player. In a dice game you can gamble anything, even a kingdom. Just invite him for a dice game and I will win his kingdom without fighting and even without shedding a single drop of blood. Stop feeling miserable because I will win everything he has got and give it to you. The entire kingdom will be yours and your revenge will be complete. But if you invite Yudhishthira yourself then surely he will not come. Better make your father invite him and I will take care of the rest."

Shakuni had been doing a sadhana of gambling. He had made special dice that he worshipped. They were almost alive and he used to talk to them. He had worked with them so much that he could play like a magician. He would rub them and then he could throw any number he wanted.*

Duryodhana started working on his father with flattery, whining and repeating, "A dice game should be arranged," and "They should be called." The king indulged his wicked sons and Duryodhana was persistent, so he always got

---

*Did you know that in India there is also a worship for Kali done by thieves before they go to steal? If the sacrifice is accepted their move will be successful.

his way. He managed to persuade his father to send Yudhishthira an invitation to come and play a game of dice.

King Dhritarashtra used to discuss everything with Vidura, the prime minister who never hesitated to tell the truth. They had the same father and all the princes addressed Vidura as uncle. Dhritarashtra knew that if Vidura conveyed the invitation to Yudhishthira he would surely come because of respect for uncle Vidura. He called his minister and said, "It has been years since the Pandavas were living here and I miss their company. Since then they've spent years building their palace and attaining the title of emperor. Now that they are well settled I would like to see them again and while they are here Yudhishthira can play a game of dice with Duryodhana. I want you to invite them for a visit to Hastinapura."

Vidura was astonished to hear this. Then he realized that it was a bunch of lies and that it was all about the game of dice. He knew Yudhishthira was fond of playing dice and Shakuni was a shrewd expert. He foresaw that Yudhishthira was going to lose. So he resisted the idea and said, "Gambling is bad; we should not encourage such games."

Dhritarashtra replied, "It is just a game and for kings; it is a good game. Let them play and enjoy. There is nothing wrong in it."

Vidura said, "If Shakuni plays with Yudhishthira, he will play tricks and cause troubles. Gambling is not good for you nor for the country and it should be avoided." Vidura contacted grandfather Bhishma and Drona who agreed that it was a bad idea, but a king is a king and especially a blind king can be obstinate, so he ignored their advice and insisted. Vidura had no other choice than to obey and go to Indraprastha as an ambassador of King Dhritarashtra. He conveyed the invitation to Yudhishthira, but he also warned him. Bhishma tried to prevent the game as well. He visited Gandhari in an attempt to undo the invitation, but it was to no avail.

The Fall of the Pandavas

In those days life had little value for a kshatriya because he always had to be prepared to fight and die. Because it was his dharma to fight he had to be ready for fighting at all times. It was a tradition for a kshatriya to accept any challenge to fight a duel or to play a game. Although everybody knew gambling was bad, no kshatriya should refuse an invitation to gamble. Yudhishthira knew he was a poor player, but as a warrior he was obliged to accept the challenge.

☗

The Dice Game

At first Yudhishthira heavily criticized gambling. He said, "Uncle, I don't want to go there because I don't trust Duryodhana. And I don't want to play dice with him because I know it is bad."

Vidura said, "I was going to tell you that, but I am glad you said it yourself."

Yudhishthira's brothers vehemently opposed the idea. They said, "Remember Duryodhana poisoned Bhima and he tried to kill us all in that house of lacquer." It was true, but Yudhishthira felt bad about Draupadi having insulted Duryodhana in Indraprastha and he felt obliged to please Duryodhana as a compensation. Also he wanted to compensate Shakuni for the loss that he had when they had played a game of dice after the inauguration ceremony.

Weaknesses create problems and even having only one weakness can cause a great problem. But weaknesses are a part of human nature. For example: after thirty years of smoking, I can tell that smoking is bad for me; even so, when I leave the house I might forget my spectacles or my passport, but I will never forget my cigarettes. Yudhishthira was a victim of his weakness for gambling. In spite of the warnings from Vidura and Bhishma, and in spite of the protests of his brothers, Yudhishthira accepted the invitation and agreed to play. At first Bhima and Arjuna refused to go, but when something has to happen it has to happen and nobody can get away from it. Even Krishna told Bhishma not to intervene in the dice game, because if it hadn't happened the whole Mahabharata would not have happened.

The five Pandava brothers and Draupadi arrived at the royal palace in Hastinapura. The brothers were given nice rooms to stay in. Draupadi was sent to the inner house where the ladies were living. Dhritarashtra called Yudhishthira and said, "It is good that you have come here. I would like you to visit the parts of the kingdom that you have not yet seen. But first you are invited to play a game of dice with my son Duryodhana."

Yudhishthira said, "I would like to ask you, my uncle, if playing dice and gambling are not considered bad things?"

The king said, "Yes gambling is bad, but if you do it just for fun and don't get seriously involved in it then it is not bad. So please be careful and don't bet anything too valuable."

Duryodhana had built a nice assembly hall for playing the dice game. Around the playground spectators could sit and watch. They could comment on the game, but they could not interfere with it. The Pandavas entered the hall, paid their homage to the people they had not seen for several years, and sat down. Then Duryodhana entered the hall. He started challenging Yudhishthira, saying, "I can play a good game and I would like to play, but you have no skills."

This was bad because it was tradition that a warrior accepted any challenge and so Yudhishthira did. He said, "I will show you that I can also play."

Then Duryodhana said, "Instead of playing myself, my uncle will play on my behalf. I will pay the money and do the transactions, but my uncle will throw the dice."

Yudhishthira said, "We both have to play our role. Why do you need somebody else to throw the dice?"

Duryodhana said, "You are afraid of his skills. You know that he is skillful. He knows how to play this game and he has command over it, so you are afraid. You are a coward. So, okay, then we won't play. Nothing wrong."

Yudhishthira said, "I am not afraid. Let me show you that I can play."

Duryodhana said, "Okay, then come on."

When the game started Vidura did not want to sit and watch and he left the hall. Yudhishthira played and lost his gold and gems. He lost his animals and servants. He lost all his villages and his whole kingdom. Then Shakuni said,

"Okay Yudhishthira, now you have lost everything, so we should stop playing."

But Yudhishthira said, "I don't want to stop playing because I expect this time I will win. So you should play and throw the dice."

Duryodhana said, "But you have nothing left. What do you now bet?"

Yudhishthira said, "Okay, I bet myself. I will become your slave if I lose."

Duryodhana agreed. Shakuni threw the dice and he won.

Duryodhana said, "Now Yudhishthira, you have become a slave. Take off your crown, take off your robes, put on simple clothes, and you will be my slave."

Yudhishthira said, "No, just a minute, I want one more chance, maybe this time I will win."

Duryodhana said, "What do you want to put up next?"

Yudhishthira said, "I bet my brother Bhima."

And Duryodhana said, "Ask him."

Yudhishthira said, "No, I am the eldest in the family and they all obey me. He will not oppose me; so play." And he lost Bhima.

Then he lost Arjuna, then he lost Nakula and Sahadeva, so finally he lost everything. Then Duryodhana said, "Okay now you have lost everything. Take off your clothes, shave your heads, be monks, and get out."

Yudhishthira said, "I still have my wife. I will wager her."

Duryodhana accepted the bet. Yudhishthira threw the dice and to the excitement of Duryodhana he lost her as well.

In Satya Yuga and Treta Yuga husband and wife had equal status but in Dvapara Yuga and Kali Yuga society became increasingly male dominated and there was less respect for the female. Yudhishthira could gamble his wife in a dice game because a wife had become property.

Draupadi's Humiliation

Duryodhana was delirious. He thought, "Now I can take revenge on Draupadi for calling me a blind son of a blind man. Now I can teach her a lesson." So he sent a messenger summoning her to the court of the king.

Draupadi refused and said she would not come because she was not feeling well. Next time the messenger went and told her to come as she was, but she refused again. The third time the man came and said, "You have been lost in the dice game and you have become a slave of King Duryodhana. If he likes he can release you. Otherwise you have to live in the palace and serve him like a maidservant. So come."

She asked him to tell her how she had been lost. Then the messenger told her that Yudhishthira had lost his wealth, his kingdom, his brothers, himself, and her. She replied that when her husband had become a slave he also had lost the right to wager her. Therefore the bet was not legal and she still refused to come. The messenger returned to Duryodhana and told him that the lady still considered herself independent because when Yudhishthira had lost himself he also had lost the right to wager her so she would not come.

Duryodhana got angry and he asked his brother Dushasana to go and bring her with force if necessary. Dushasana went to her room, grabbed her long hair, and dragged her to the court. Bhima got so angry that he could have killed Dushasana, but Yudhishthira said, "We are bound by words and the bondage is created by us. We have to do what we say and because we have said that we are slaves we have no right to protest and fight. When the time is right we will fight, but at the moment we cannot." It was only because Yudhishthira was a very just person that he could keep Bhima under control.

Duryodhana wanted to show the Pandavas that they had lost everything and they had become worthless, so he ordered Draupadi to come and sit on his lap. To say that to a married lady in front of her husband is an insult. Bhima was feeling so bad that he could have killed Duryodhana at that time. He took a vow saying, "You have told Draupadi to sit on your lap and you will see that I am going to break your thigh for that." He talked bluntly, but at that moment he could not do much because he was bound by the words of his eldest brother to be a slave without the right to protest.

Yudhishthira's brothers were perfectly obedient and they had great forgiveness. No ordinary brother would accept their brother bartering away their freedom in a dice game, but they did. Yudhishthira tried to update the old values and to establish the rule of dharma because he was a son of Dharma. By his nature he judged everything from the ultimate point of view and never judged on the spot. He really saw future connotations of any decision he made. Nevertheless he made several mistakes. His decision to play with Duryodhana was wrong and betting people who had the right to decide about themselves without permission was also wrong.

Draupadi was standing helpless without the protection of her mighty husbands. She said, "Don't talk like this, Duryodhana."

Then Karna said, "You don't have the right to talk because you are a slave."

She said, "But I was bet by a person who had already lost himself, so he did not have the right to wager me." Everybody refused to listen to her.

She approached Bhishma, the great grandfather, and said, "You are seeing something wrong is happening here and you are silent?"

Bhishma said, "I told them long back this is all wrong, but they don't listen to me. I cannot do anything."

She said, "Then why don't you get away from here?" He said, "Because I would still be bound by my vow to protect Hastinapura."

Then she addressed Drona, Kripa, and all the other great people there, but nobody helped her.

Draupadi said to Duryodhana, "I am not your slave and I will not obey you," to which Duryodhana said, "Take off her clothes and then she will know who has authority."

Dushasana grabbed her sari and started pulling. Many brave and righteous people were there, but nobody interfered. It was only one piece of cloth, so it should take only a few seconds to undress her.* Draupadi thought, "I cannot expect any help from the people here. I should ask god." She called upon Krishna and said, "Lord help me, these people are harassing me."

---

*Indian ladies wear a sari, which is a single piece of cloth five yards long. It has no zipper, button, or clasp, and is elegantly wrapped around the body. If it is pulled, it will come off.

Dushasana pulled the sari and Draupadi went round and round, but her sari kept on becoming longer and longer. Draupadi thought only about Krishna while Dushasana kept on pulling the cloth. It kept piling up and slowly it filled the court. This continued until Dushasana got exhausted and collapsed. He fell down and could not pull any more. All the great warriors, teachers, and advocates of dharma saw the miracle happening. Bhishma, the great warrior and follower of dharma, Drona, the great teacher, and Ashvatthama, the warrior, were all quiet because they were terrified by the wickedness of Duryodhana. They felt weak because the evil force appeared so strong. They lacked the courage to challenge the evil.

Draupadi rearranged her sari. She was furious. She asked everybody why Duryodhana had been allowed to insult her like that, but nobody could tell her. She approached the blind king and his wife. She said, "You have disrespected a respectable woman, which will bring you suffering and destruction. I curse your coming generation."

Dhritarashtra got up and said, "Draupadi, what happened was wrong and our children were wrong, but please do not curse them. They are stupid. I am the king and I free you and give you back everything that you have lost. I free your husbands and I give them back the kingdom. So now you all have your freedom and your kingdom back. Pick up your things and go home. This game is over. From the very beginning I knew it was not right. I am blind, so I could not see it, but I could hear that there was a great dishonor to my daughter-in-law. My sons have disrespected the family, they have done wrong, so they will suffer."

Everybody was silent. The five brothers picked up their arms, their robes, and crowns and walked out of the court and went home. Duryodhana got up and said to his father, "I protest against your interference. Yudhishthira bet his wife, his brothers, and his kingdom by his own free will and nobody compelled him. You should not have given everything back to him. Only because you are my father I accept it." He left the hall and the court was suspended.

———◆———

Going into Exile

The wicked Duryodhana felt bad because just a minute before he had the entire kingdom, the Pandava brothers had become his slaves, and Draupadi his maidservant. His father unnecessarily had been generous and given it all back. He did not want to lose it all so easily. Duryodhana went to his father and said, "I am sorry for all that happened. I was angry and full of hatred toward Draupadi because she had abused you and insulted me. Because of that anger and hatred I acted wrongly, but I didn't really want anything bad. Now they have their kingdom back. But it does not feel completely right, so I would like to invite them to play one final game."

Dhritarashtra said, "No more games, it only brings problems."

Duryodhana started whining, "Please, Papa, I will never ask you for anything again. Please let me call them back to play a final game. Before we played for goods and people and that created problems. But the final game should have a different stake. The loser has to live in the forest for twelve years and people may know his whereabouts, but the thirteenth year he has to go into hiding so that nobody knows where he is. Should his whereabouts become disclosed then the loser again has to go in exile for thirteen years."

Duryodhana was relying on the expertise of his uncle Shakuni. He was confident that if Yudhishthira would come back to play once more he would lose again. He thought that an exile in the forest would be almost as effective at getting the Pandavas out of his way as killing them. When they were in the forest he would rule over the kingdom. And in the year when they had to live anonymously he would send his spies out to find them and surely they would succeed because the Pandavas were extraordinary wherever they were. And then they would have to go in exile for thirteen years again. That way they would never come out of exile and he would have the entire kingdom for himself.

The poor blind king could not refuse his son anything. So the Pandavas were called back just before they left for Indraprastha. Everybody was against another game. But as it had to happen, so it had to happen. Yudhishthira accepted the challenge to sit down and gamble again.

That was another mistake Yudhishthira made because of his attachment to gambling. Gambling is one of the worst things. It is taking risks at the cost of anything, entertaining challenges, and doing wrong things.

Everybody told Yudhishthira not to play again, but he did not listen. And of course he lost again. They all had to take off their robes and crowns and dress like jungle people. They were allowed to take their arms to the forest. They had to live in the forest for twelve years and then one more year without being found. Meanwhile Duryodhana would rule both Hastinapura and Indraprastha while Dhritarashtra was king only in name.

———◆———

Destiny and the Name of the Lord

When Vidura warned the king and everybody involved that the dice game would bring disaster to the whole clan, nobody listened. It seems fatalistic to say that it happened because it had to happen, but Kali Yuga was coming and an end had to come to the power accumulated in people through hard work, regular exercises, martial arts, and practicing of dharma. Many times the circumstances have been prepared in such a way that it is difficult to change the course of events. Similarly, we continue our way of life although we know it is dangerous to destroy the environment. In spite of all the conferences on ecology every year the consumption of nonrecyclable articles increases.

How come a poor football team like Denmark beat Germany while Holland lost to them? It is destiny. I was in Germany and a Dutch friend of mine was there also. Lots of people prayed to god that if the Dutch did not win the Germans also should not win, so "let the Danes be victorious." On TV I saw the German team in some concentration camp surrounded with barbwire. The wife and son of one of the players came up to the barbwire and the player came from the other side, but the coach did not allow him to go out and comfort his crying son. They had to stay in the camp for twenty days, all the time thinking about football only. How is it possible that they lost? And the Danish guys were coming from a two-week vacation and did not even know that they were going to enter into the World Cup finals. How is it possible that they won? It all happens because it has to happen. Even if you had replaced the Danish team by twelve elephants the ball would still have gone in the German goal because it had to happen.

Just as Vidura tried to prevent the dice game even when he knew it was inevitable, I know that you have no time to make fresh food and chapattis every day, but still I talk about it and I hope that someday some people will do it. That is a part of the game. Lots of books about good health and good life are coming out. The writers know that nobody can follow all their advice, but still they write those books. Some people, like Jehovah's Witnesses, continue talking although they know that nobody is listening. In the same way, in your life your friends give lots of advice to you, but you don't believe them and do whatever you like. All the things told to you by others make no sense to you; any change has to happen from within.

Mahabharata tells us that even if we are told the truth we will still continue doing what is destined for us to do. Destiny plays an important role in life. And the only thing that helps is the name of god.

Krishna's Many Names

When Dushasana was pulling her sari, Draupadi called Krishna by many names and it took him a long time to come and help. But when she concentrated on one name he immediately appeared as the sari that became infinite. Some time later Draupadi asked Krishna, "Why did it take so long for you to come while I was afraid that the guy would make me naked?"

And Krishna said, "Well sister, the problem is that at that time you were calling me by a hundred names. First you called Murari and I had to run to Vrindavan to put the flute on my lips and become Murari. Then you called Giridhari and I had to run from Vrindavan to Govardhan to hold up the mountain over the kingdom. And then you called Gopala, so I ran from Govardhan to Mathura to take care of the cows. Then you called Dvarakanath and I had to run from Mathura to Dvaraka to become Dvarakanath. So you did not let me rest anywhere. Each time I had to change my costume and my makeup before I could come and that took time. If you had only called me by one name I would have been there immediately."

Draupadi said, "Okay, next time when I call you I will only use one name." He said, "I will be right there."

———◆———

When you are in trouble remember the one who removes all troubles. He is kind and his games are infinite. Although he has many names and although all forms are his form, just remember only one name and only one form. This is a good lesson in Mahabharata that there can be a hundred names for the energy that you want to deal with, but if you take the name that is the most suitable at that moment then your job can be done easily.

14

Forest Exile

Rishi Durvasa is famous in Indian culture and he appears in many stories and in the famous drama of Shakuntala written by Kalidasa, which inspired Goethe to write Faust. Durvasa curses lady Shakuntala, "As you were not paying attention to me, so your husband will forget you." That starts a series of problems in her life. Rishi Durvasa was the same rishi who cursed Ganga to be born on Earth and who taught Kunti the mantra to receive a son from any god. The next story is about the rishi visiting Kunti's sons.

Durvasa Visits the Pandavas

In the first year that the Pandavas lived in exile in the forest Rishi Durvasa happened to visit Duryodhana in the royal palace of Hastinapura. Duryodhana was never good to saints, but to Durvasa he behaved humbly and he did his best to make a feast for him. When the rishi was about to leave he said, "I am happy with you Duryodhana. Tell me what you want."

Duryodhana said, "Please bless my cousins who are living in the forest and visit them with all your disciples." He knew that the rishi was likely to get angry quickly and then give curses. The Pandavas were living in exile in sober conditions without money. To cook food they had to collect wood from the forest. Surely the rishi staying with his disciples at their house would embarrass them and might even cause their destruction. Next day Durvasa and his two hundred disciples went to the forest. When they arrived at the place of the Pandavas he said, "I am going to take a bath in the river nearby with my disciples. When we come back we will be hungry so you can start making food now."

Yudhishthira said, "Okay, sir," and then the rishi and his disciples went to the river. Surya, the sun god, had given the Pandavas a special pot (akshayapatra) to be used for cooking. Once a day it would feed everybody present, no matter how many people. But when everybody was fed and the pot had been cleaned it would not work again until the next day. Duryodhana had arranged that Durvasa would arrive late when everybody had eaten and the pot had been cleaned. The Pandavas were in trouble; there was no food in the house. And because they were living in the jungle there were no neighbors to go to and ask for ingredients to prepare food and entertain their guests.

Whenever Draupadi got nervous she remembered Krishna. She said, "Lord, we are in trouble. I have to prepare dinner for Durvasa and his disciples, but we have finished all the food for today."

Krishna appeared and said, "Draupadi, I am hungry, bring me some food."

She said, "But that is the problem! At the moment Durvasa and his disciples are taking baths, but they can come back here any moment. And then I have to feed two hundred people, but we haven't got any more food today. I don't know what to do."

Krishna said, "Bring me the pot."

She said, "But I washed it and there is nothing in it."

He said, "Bring it anyway and let me see." So Draupadi brought the pot and behind the rim Krishna found a small grain of rice, which Draupadi had overlooked. He said, "That will do." Krishna took it and said, "Spirit of the universe that makes everybody hungry and satisfies everybody's hunger, I offer you this grain of rice. Let it satisfy the hunger of everybody in the universe." He put the grain in his mouth and ate it with appreciation.

Durvasa and the disciples who were taking bath started burping. Their stomachs were bloating full of food, so they left the water. They could not even

think about food. Draupadi and the five brothers were waiting, but nobody
showed up. They sent Bhima to the river to find out what was happening.
The rishi told him, "Listen, I am so full that I cannot move and I will not eat
any more today. Thank you very much and I am sorry for having troubled
you. God bless you." That way god managed to help the Pandavas at the last
moment and Duryodhana's plan failed to hurt them. During their exile they
were able to entertain all people who came around and even live like kings.

Yudhishthira's Wisdom

When the Pandavas were living in the forest a deer took the churning stick
away from a group of brahmins that needed the stick to make fire for their
fire worship (homa). The brahmins came to the Pandavas and asked them to
bring back their churning stick from the deer that had run away with it in its
antlers. The Pandavas chased the deer, but when it disappeared they all sat
down. After running through the forest for hours they felt thirsty.

Yudhishthira asked Nakula and Sahadeva to fetch some water from a
nearby pond. But when the twins wanted to take water from the pond a voice
said, "Answer my questions or you cannot drink water here." The voice was
from a nature spirit (yaksha) that was guarding the pond.

The twins did not listen. They took some water and dropped dead. After
some time Bhima was sent to search for the twins and get some water. When
Bhima also did not return, Arjuna went.

Finally Yudhishthira had to go and see for himself. He found the four
brothers lying dead near the pond. The voice said, "If you try to drink from my
water without answering my questions you will also die."

Yudhishthira agreed. The yaksha asked him questions and Yudhishthira
gave profound answers. One of the questions was, "What is the most
astonishing thing in this world?"

Yudhishthira replied, "The most astonishing thing in this world is that
everybody is dying around us and yet nobody is thinking that he will also die."

When Yudhishthira had answered all the questions the spirit was satisfied and said, "You may choose which one of the four I will bring back to life." When Yudhishthira chose Nakula the spirit asked, "Why do you select this one when the others are so powerful and intelligent?"

Yudhishthira replied, "I select him because I am one from one mother and he is one from the other mother. This way at least one son from each mother will be alive."* This impressed the spirit so much that he revived all four.

———◆———

ᐧᐁᐧ

Pilgrimages to Holy Places

When the Pandavas were living in the forest waiting for twelve years to pass they had nothing special to do. Brahmins and saints were visiting them and Lomash Rishi was one of the regular visitors.† He told them, "If you stay in one place many useless people will surround you and because you are royal in nature, you will take care of them, bring them food, arrange their comfort, and your life will be wasted. Go on a pilgrimage to visit shrines and holy places."

The Pandavas asked him to take them around because no one else knew more about holy places than he. He even knew about places that had been holy in previous creations. He agreed and for a couple of years he guided them around the holy places of India and explained their significance. He showed them the places of Vishnu's incarnations as a lion, a boar, and as a dwarf. He explained the importance of Haridwar, Varanasi, and Sagara. He told them about the important places in the Himalayas and all the ashrams and the rishis who had lived there. As the Mahabharata describes their pilgrimage and all the stories of the holy places and power spots of India, it gives a picture of the holy places in India of six thousand years ago.

———◆———

---

*Nakula and Sahadeva were sons of Madri, but if Kunti would have loved them any less than her own sons, Yudhishthira would have chosen Bhima or Arjuna.

†Lomash Rishi, who was also known as the hairy rishi, was a great saint who appears in the Mahabharata, the Puranas, and other texts.

The following story breaks the limited consciousness of people who want to live for a hundred years.

The Lifetime of Lomash Rishi

Lomash Rishi was born in the beginning of this cycle of creation (kalpa). After he prayed to god for a long time he heard a voice saying, "I am happy with your worship. Ask me for a boon."

Lomash said, "Make me immortal."

The voice said, "Everything changes and nothing can remain forever. Change is the law of nature. One who takes birth also has to die. Even Indra and Brahma have to die; in one lifetime of Brahma fourteen Indras die. Nobody is immortal and I cannot grant you immortality. But you can ask me for the longest span of life that you can think of."

Lomash Rishi said, "Please give me a boon that when one Brahma dies one of my hairs will fall off. And only when all of my hairs have fallen off will I die."

———◆———

If you consider that there are about 33 million hair pores on the body then it is possible to figure out the life span of Lomash Rishi. One day of Brahma consists of one cycle of creation and destruction. Early in the morning of his day Brahma creates the world and before he goes to bed he destroys it again. A night of Brahma follows, which lasts an equal length of time. Together they are considered to last 8.6 million solar years. One year of Brahma is 365 such days and one lifetime of Brahma is 100 years. Thus the life of one Brahma is: 33 million x 8.6 million x 365 x 100 = 10 million million million years.

In India old and young live together in the same house. There old people want to live long to have good times with their grandchildren and pass on their experience; their age feels like a boon for the grandchildren and people bless them to live long. But in the West old age has become a curse. It causes panic and problems because old people are kept separate in old people's homes where they are waiting for death. Once a week you bring them flowers bought only for them and packed beautifully with lots of paper and garbage around them. Or you bring them fruits and at the most you take a cup of tea from the old people's home, but there is no further contact. That version of old age creates terror and that's why Westerners don't want to live long. But if you were told you could live the same way as you are today then I think you would like to grow old. Lomash Rishi was a yogi who could live the way he wanted, so he wanted a long life.

15
Devayani and Kacha

When the Pandavas were exiled from their kingdom brahmins and saints used to visit them and tell them stories according to how they were feeling at the time, such as stories to help them get over nervousness or depression. One of those stories is about Devayani and Kacha (according to Indian tradition the lady is mentioned first).

Shukra Revives the Demons

Brihaspati (Jupiter) was the son of Rishi Angira. Shukra (Venus) was the son of Prabhu, a great saint and a rishi.* Both Brihaspati and Shukra came from good families and they were class fellows. Brihaspati mastered the spiritual sciences and was most interested in knowledge, divine pursuits, worship, and meditation. Because he did not go for worldly pleasures he had not made much fortune. Shukra on the other hand loved dance and the company of beautiful people and he had a few bad habits like drinking liquor and eating meat, which prevented him from reaching the same spiritual height as Brihaspati. That made him feel inferior. His father was a rishi who remembered all the

---

*While in Western mythology the moon and Venus are female, in Indian mythology both are male and the moon even has twenty-seven wives.

129

scriptures by heart and he had asked his son to write them down. Because Shukra had spent time writing scriptures and his genetic information came from a rishi, he knew all the scriptures. He thought that knowing the scriptures was enough whereas Brihaspati not only knew them but also practiced them.

When Shiva had to appoint a teacher of the gods (devas) he decided to give the post to Brihaspati because he always strictly followed the law of dharma whereas Shukra sometimes drank liquor and created problems in the neighborhood, which is inappropriate for a teacher of the gods. Shukra became angry because he had expected to be appointed. In knowledge and in lineage he was equal to Brihaspati. In karma he was not, but nobody cared about that and social status was the thing that mattered most. Shukra wanted to take revenge and joined the opposite camp to become the teacher of the demons (asuras).

To show Brihaspati he could do better, Shukra worshipped Shiva in the special form of Mahamrityunjaya, which knows the mantra to conquer death; from Mahamrityunjaya Shukra gained the power to revive the dead (sanjivini vidya). Brihaspati knew the art of healing wounds, consoling the spirit, and bringing peace to life, but the power of bringing the dead back to life made Shukra more powerful than Brihaspati. The gods and the demons were natural enemies and they were fighting a grim war about who would rule over the three worlds: heaven, Earth, and the underworld. During the day lots of demons would get killed by the gods, but in the evening Shukra would come, chant the mantra, sprinkle water over the dead bodies, and then they would all get up as fresh as before. The next day the gods would come to the battlefield and see all the demons alive again and that demoralized them.

The Demons Kill Kacha

Shiva scarcely teaches anybody anything and after teaching the secret science to Shukra he refused to teach the sanjivini vidya to the gods because then everybody would start reviving the dead. The gods decided that somebody should go and learn the secret mantra from Shukra. When they thought about who could do it they agreed that the most humble, the most beautiful, the most honest and charming person in the entire kingdom of gods was Kacha, the son of Brihaspati. He was a brahmachari. He was charming by manners and physical appearance. He was well behaved, honorable, and nice.

The gods thought that Shukra would burn anyone else with the fire of his tapasya but Kacha might win over his heart and learn the secret from him. Then the handicap of the gods would be neutralized. Kacha agreed and he went to Shukra's home in the capital of the demon kingdom. He greeted the teacher appropriately and introduced himself, "I am Kacha, grandson of the holy wise man Angira and son of Brihaspati. I am a brahmachari who is thirsty for knowledge under your guidance."

According to the law a wise teacher could not refuse a dignified student who asked for his guidance and knowledge, so Shukra consented to the request. He said, "Kacha, you come from a good family. I accept you as my student even more because by accepting you I also show my respect to Brihaspati. He is the teacher of gods and I am the teacher of demons. I will teach you anything you want except the sanjivini vidya. That is my secret and I keep it for demons only."

Kacha studied many years under the guidance of Shukra. He flawlessly performed the obligatory tasks in the household of his master. After Shukra's wife had passed away he had nobody left except a graceful daughter called Devayani whom he loved deeply. Kacha did his best to entertain her with singing, dancing, and playing. He managed to win her affection without breaking his vow of brahmachari.

At first the demons did not know Kacha and they did not worry. But when they found out he was the son of Brihaspati they suspected he had come to steal the secret of sanjivini vidya from Shukra, which would be a disaster. One day when Kacha was tending his master's cows the demons assaulted him, tore his body to pieces, and fed them to the dogs. When the cows returned home without Kacha, Devayani got worried and she went to her father, lamenting, "The sun has set and the evening puja has passed, but still Kacha has not returned home. The cows have come back without him. I am afraid something terrible has happened to him. Oh, I can't live without him."

The loving father used his knowledge of sanjivini and commanded the young man to appear. Immediately Kacha came back to life and, smiling, he greeted his master. When Devayani asked him why he had stayed out so long he told her that he had been tending the cows when suddenly the demons had assaulted him. How he had come back to life he did not remember, but he was all right. Another day Kacha went to the field to pick flowers for Devayani and again the demons killed him. This time they pounded his body to a paste and dissolved it in the sea.

When he had not returned home, even after a long time, Devayani went to her father again. He revived Kacha again by the sanjivini vidya and he heard what had happened. The demons got scared because Shukra revived Kacha each time. They tried their best to be more clever and conceived the idea of killing the boy and hiding him inside Shukra's body where he would not be found. They organized a big feast in the palace of the demon king Vrishaparva and invited Shukra. Just before the beginning of the feast they killed Kacha, burned his body, mixed the ashes with liquor, and during the feast they gave the liquor to Shukra who drank it without knowing the addition.

When Kacha did not come back Devayani started crying and once again she went to her father complaining about Kacha staying out. Shukra tried to console his daughter. He said, "I have revived Kacha already twice and it seems the demons really want to get rid of him. Instead of me reviving him over and over again you had better learn to live without him. Death comes for everybody someday and wise men should not lament about that. You still have an entire life to enjoy youth, beauty, and everybody's friendship." But Devayani loved Kacha deeply and since the beginning of time good counsel never eased an aching heart.

She replied, "Kacha, grandson of Angira and son of Brihaspati, was an impeccable boy who was completely devoted to our service. I love him with all my might and now that he is gone life has become grim and worthless for me; therefore I will follow him."

Shukra was hurt by the grief of his daughter and once again he used his sanjivini power to summon Kacha back to life. But Kacha was still dispersed in the wine inside Shukra's body. He was in an awkward condition and could not come out. When his name was called he only could reply from inside Shukra's body.

Shukra said, "Where are you Kacha?"

Kacha replied, "I am in your belly." Amazed and annoyed, Shukra asked, "How did you get inside of me?"

Then Kacha told him everything in detail in spite of his uncomfortable position.

Shukra became angry with the demons. He felt like choosing the side of the gods. He said, "Liquor is such a bad thing that I give a curse. From today onward any brahmin drinking liquor will lose his consciousness."

He said to the demons, "I was not going to tell him the secret science, but now I must because of your distrust. I have to bring him back to life because I don't want my daughter to be sad and I don't want to digest Brihaspati's son. But when he comes back to life he has to pierce my stomach and I will die. Therefore I will have to teach him the mantra first so that he can bring me back to life. That is the only possibility. From today onward I am not going to help you anymore because you did not trust me."

Shukra taught Kacha the mantra. And when Kacha came out of Shukra's body the great teacher was ripped to pieces and dropped dead. But immediately Kacha revived him with the newly learned mantra. Kacha bowed before Shukra and said, "The teacher who gives an ignorant person a share of knowledge is like a father and because I came from your body now you are also my mother." Kacha had come there to learn the mantra. Now the job was done and he could return to his father.

He took leave of his teacher and he was about to return to the world of the gods. He had no reason to hang around Devayani; actually she was hanging around him. In those days it was not unusual that a brahmin woman spoke freely about marrying. Devayani said, "Oh grandson of Angira, in my heart I admire your impeccable life, your great accomplishments, and your noble birth. I have loved you for a long time with tenderness even though you were true to your vow of brahmachari. Will you now answer my love and marry me? Brihaspati and you deserve to be honored by me."

But Kacha replied, "You are my master's daughter and deserve my respect. I got back life by being born from your father's body, so I am your brother and you are my sister. Marrying you would not be appropriate."

Devayani tried to convince him in vain, "You are the son of Brihaspati and not of my father. It is not appropriate that you leave behind somebody like me who is without blame and completely devoted to you. I have always loved you and longed for you as my husband. Please stay."

Kacha replied, "Don't try to persuade me to act wrongly. You are attractive and when you are angry you are even more attractive. But I am your brother, so bid me farewell."

With these words Kacha detached himself from her. Then she got really sad and she cursed him, "Because you desert me without marrying me you will not be able to use this knowledge." So from that day Kacha could not use the mantra. Shukra had to comfort his daughter and after some time she managed to forget Kacha.

———◆———

Demons and Gods Inside

The demons represent our feelings of sensual enjoyment, which are ruled by Venus. And the gods represent the feelings of oneness with divinity and higher consciousness. When the divine feelings defeat the demonic feelings Venus revives the demons. Even after a long time of doing hard work and penance, you still cannot be sure that the demons inside are killed forever. After twenty-five years of working as a celibate, you may think you have overcome the demon of sensuality, but Venus will revive it if you don't keep on practicing. But, on the other hand, if you lose your divine feelings you cannot pick them up again where you lost them because of Devayani's curse.

More demons are coming all the time. They are wearing good clothes, driving big cars, living the good life, and they have credit cards now. If you search for god you need a torch or an electronic detector that makes a sound when god is near. The race of gods is annihilated because of ladies controlling birth with pills that disturb their hormone system. Demons and humans are alive, but gods are there no more. But we can still bring them back to life.

16

Arjuna in Heaven

In the Hindu way of thinking life exists at seven levels. In my book *Leela** and in my book on *Chakras,* these levels of existence are discussed: the *bhu loka* (physical plane), the *bhuvar loka* (astral plane), the *svarga loka* (heavenly plane), the *maha loka* (plane of balance), the *jana loka* (human plane), the *tapah loka* (plane of austerity), and the *satya loka* (reality plane). The seven levels are inside and outside of the body. At the first three levels life can be seen, but at four levels it is beyond perception. So life exists at different levels and in different forms, sometimes visible sometimes invisible. But visible and invisible are only two states of consciousness; something visible can become invisible and something invisible can become visible.

Heaven is a third-chakra concept. People think of heaven (svarga loka, celestial abode, paradise) as a place of enjoyment. It does not matter if you are having problems with your body on Earth. It may be fat, thin, tall, or small; or you may have problems with your eyes or ears, or problems in talking and communication, but in heaven all those problems are gone. There everybody can sing, dance, enjoy, and communicate. There is no inhibition, no prohibition, and everybody is free. Every

---

The Yoga of Snakes and Arrows: The Leela of Self-Knowledge (Rochester, Vt.: Destiny Books, 2007).

prophet promises he will take you to heaven if you do good karma, fight for his army, or believe in him. But only the few real believers will be allowed into heaven and the rest will go to hell. Everyone thinks, "There will be a big crowd in hell, but surely we will be in heaven."

The next story from Mahabharata is famous and there is also a classical theater play about Pururavas written by Bhas. It has beautiful dialogues showing how stupid a man gets when he is taken over by the desire for pleasure and gratification of the senses.

◦❦◦

Urvashi and Pururavas

Indra, the king of heaven, was always afraid that somebody else would acquire enough power to take his place. If anybody was becoming too powerful he used to send his army of celestial nymphs to seduce the person and destroy his tapasya. These nymphs always remained sixteen years of age and they lived in heaven without children or husband. Even if they married they belonged to nobody. If they got pregnant they had to live on Earth until they had given birth. The leader of this army was Kama or Cupid, the god of sex. Mostly he joined the nymphs, but sometimes he was busy elsewhere and the nymphs were sent out without him.

Urvashi was the most beautiful and most charming nymph, so whenever somebody was becoming invincible she was sent to seduce him. Most of the time she was successful in breaking the tapasya, but a couple of times she failed and got cursed. Once Rishi Vasishta was moving around in heaven dressed like a saint; at that time and place he looked out of place. When Urvashi laughed at him he cursed her to live on Earth for one year as a worldly woman. Indra directed her to a powerful king called Pururavas.

King Pururavas was moving around in a forest in a good mood when he saw Urvashi. He fell in love with her and requested her to marry him. She said, "I am a celestial being, I cannot marry a man who lives on Earth. I cannot be your wife because after one year I will have to go back to heaven."

The king thought, "One year is 365 days, that is quite a lot." So he said, "I don't care about next year. Right now, right here I want to marry you. Who cares what happens after one year, that is too much. Please marry me right now."

She said, "We could live together without me being your wife."

He said, "I am a man who has to do a ceremony to get sanction from the society for living with you."

She consented and he brought her to his kingdom. They married and started living together. The king thought that 365 days and nights was quite a lot, but they passed like a moment. And one morning when the king woke up he found the garment of the nymph on the bed, but she had gone. Pururavas started running around madly, crying out loud, "Urvashi, where are you?"

But Urvashi was unkind; she had no love or attachment to anybody. She had been cursed to stay on Earth for a year and she only had to pass her time. She found good company and had some fun. After that she was not interested in him anymore and she went home, leaving Pururavas suffering.

Urvashi Curses Arjuna

Arjuna had expert knowledge of archery, but Bhishma and Drona, who were loyal to Duryodhana, had all the knowledge of working with divine weapons, Bhishma because he had been educated in heaven and Drona because he was an expert in martial arts. They had the divine weapons—Brahma astra, Vishnu astra, and Narayana astra—which bring total destruction in no time. They also had the Mohan astra, which puts the enemy into a state of hypnotic trance. In case of a fight these weapons would overpower the Pandavas unless Arjuna was better equipped. So Krishna told him he should go to the Himalayas and gather divine weapons from Shiva, the lord of destruction, who had all weapons.

Arjuna agreed. He left his brothers in the forest and went to the Himalayas. There he sat down and meditated on Shiva many days, but nothing happened. One day he was confronted with a wild boar that tried to attack him. Arjuna picked up his bow and shot an arrow to defend himself. At the same time *another arrow came from somewhere else and it felled the boar. Arjuna felt offended because he thought that he was the best archer of the world. Who else had the courage to shoot an arrow on anything that he shot? He looked around and shouted a challenge and then a man from the Kirata tribe showed up.**

The Kirata man said, "I shot the other arrow."

Arjuna did not recognize him as Shiva; he said, "But the boar died with my arrow."

Both claimed to have killed the boar and they started a fight to decide who was the best. Arjuna relied on his bow, Gandhiva, but he could not beat the Kirata man. He thought, "Who can be so powerful?"

Then he closed his eyes and meditated on Shiva. When he opened his eyes he found Shiva standing in front of him saying, "I took the form of a Kirata and I came to test you. Now I am happy with you and I will give you all the divine weapons you need. But there are some weapons that I have given to Indra. They are in his custody and they can only be gotten from him. Because he is your father he will give them to you, but you will have to go to heaven."

In heaven there exists some subtle kind of body called sambhogakaya *and one can enjoy it. In heaven there is pleasure. But the physical body, which enjoys sensual pleasures through work organs and sense organs, does not exist in heaven. So in heaven enjoyment on a second chakra level does not mean a physical indulgence. If you go to heaven you have to leave your body on Earth. But Arjuna stayed in heaven as a human being with his body. It was one of the most adventurous parts of his life.*

When Arjuna had arrived in heaven he was sent to Vishvakarma, the divine architect who made the most powerful weapons. Vishvakarma showed him all the weapons he had created and he taught him how to use them, which took about a year because it was not so easy. In the meantime Arjuna also learned dancing, singing, and lots of secret mantras from Kitusain, a celestial singer (gandharva). Arjuna also spent much time with the daughter of Kitusain.

---

*The Kirata wear feathers like American Indians. The cover of my book *Tools for Tantra* (Rochester, Vt.: Destiny Books, 1988) shows Shiva and Shakti dressed as a Kirata man and woman. Kalidasa has written a book called *Kirata arjuni.*

Arjuna lived happily in heaven, almost forgetting time. He enjoyed life as an ordinary man in a heavenly atmosphere where everything was available.

One year passed and Arjuna was still busy when the nymph Urvashi came. She liked Arjuna and she requested him to be her friend and give her company. Arjuna replied, "This is difficult for me because you have been the wife of my great grandfather, King Pururavas."

Urvashi tried to convince Arjuna, saying, "Your visa is just for a couple of months, so you are not here forever and I am not with anybody forever, so why don't we have a good time?"

Arjuna was still in his human body and if he had gone with Urvashi he would have physically indulged in it. That's why she wanted it. But Arjuna politely refused, saying, "Grandma, I am sorry."

Urvashi was hurt. She was a young ever-green girl who had never been refused by anybody in her life. Even great rishis and saints had become crazy about her when they saw her. They all wanted to get together with her. She said, "I give you a curse. Because you refused me I take your male power away and you will be impotent."

Arjuna said, "If I go back home without my male power I will be in big trouble because I have two wives. If I had only Draupadi I could say my four brothers will take care of her. But I also have Subhadra who is my wife alone and this will cause too much trouble. Grandma, please understand my situation. I will go crazy. Remember that you once married my great grandfather and lived as a wife, so please be kind to me, I am your child."

But she said, "In our relationship there is no man, no woman, and no child. We don't believe in that, we believe only in being together. And if you don't do that you must suffer."

Arjuna went to Indra, his father, and said, "Papa, Granny has given me a curse; what should I do?"

Indra said, "I will take care of it. You need this kind of curse. You will see it will be useful to you."

Indra went to Urvashi and said, "You shouldn't be so crazy. Time and again we have punished you for being crazy like this and you always go to extremes and do wrong things. Why did you do that?"

She said, "He is such a beautiful man, I like him. You get all kinds of beautiful persons and I can't touch them or even talk to them? That is no good. I am here to entertain, but I also have a heart. I like him."

Indra replied, "But you liked his grandfather."

She said, "I liked his grandfather and I like him too."

He said, "Oh come on, be kind and do something good for him; he is your child."

She said, "Okay, on your request I withdraw my curse; but because nothing can be withdrawn completely, I will make it time-bound. He will be impotent and live without any sex for one year. And I give him a choice that he can do it whenever he wants to do it. Is that alright?"

Indra said, "Thank you, that is very helpful."

Indra went to Arjuna and said, "Listen, I got you a boon. It was a curse, but I got it changed so that it will really be a boon to you. You will need it. At the time when you have to live one year anonymously and nobody should know who you are, you can choose to be a eunuch or a woman. I have arranged your exile inside a palace where nobody will find you. Nobody will ever think that such a warrior and beautiful male like you could become a eunuch or a lady. But you can do it because of the curse and that way it has become a boon for you. Now your apprenticeship is over. Get your weapons together and go back home, otherwise somebody else will come around and create new problems for you. Heaven is not a good place for you, so you should never try to apply for a visa for heaven again." Then Arjuna returned to Earth.

———◆———

Coming Out of Exile

The curse from Urvashi to become impotent helped Arjuna to live for a year as lady Brihannala in the palace of King Virata, where he taught princess Uttara dancing and singing. Without the curse it would have been difficult for him to hide himself from the eyes of Duryodhana and remain safe. It had been agreed that if the Pandavas were not discovered during the thirteenth year of exile they would get their kingdom back. But when the year was over and they came back from their exile,

Duryodhana said that they had no claim on Indraprastha because they had lost it in the dice game, and if they really wanted it they would have to fight for it.

The greedy Duryodhana claimed the kingdom that did not belong to him. Because the Pandavas had been in exile for thirteen years they did not have the power to take back their kingdom. At first the Pandavas wanted to avoid war because war is bad and destructive. They devised a compromise to keep the peace. Krishna proposed to Duryodhana that he give the five brothers five small villages instead of their kingdom. Each Pandava would rule one village and live on its revenues. But Duryodhana even refused to give them a needlepoint of land. If the Pandavas wanted any land they had to fight for it. War between the Pandavas and the Kauravas became unavoidable.

17

Preparations for War

In the conflict between the Pandavas and the Kauravas all neighboring kingdoms got involved as well. Both sides started asking the kings of various countries to send an army to help them. Those who thought that the Pandavas were honest and right and that injustice had been done to them joined their side. Other kings joined the side of the Kauravas.

Duryodhana and Arjuna Seek Krishna's Support

Duryodhana and Arjuna both went to Dvaraka where Krishna was king to ask for his help. Duryodhana entered Krishna's room a little before Arjuna and he saw that Krishna was asleep, so he had to wait. With pride he sat down comfortably on a chair near Krishna's head. When Arjuna entered the room he remained humbly standing near Krishna's feet, waiting for Krishna to tell him to sit down. For a devotee (bhakta), the feet of the beloved are auspicious and holy, so Arjuna was showing his respect to Krishna by standing at his feet.

When Krishna opened his eyes he saw Arjuna first and he said, "Hello, Arjuna, how are you? When did you come?"

Arjuna said, "Just now."

Then Krishna saw Duryodhana and said, "You are also here?"

Duryodhana said, "Yes, I came before Arjuna."

Krishna said, "What brings both of you here at the same time?"

Duryodhana said, "War cannot be avoided, so we are now requesting kings of the neighboring countries to participate. We have come here to ask you with whom you are going to be. Those who like me are invited to support my side."

Krishna said, "My position is odd. I cannot choose either side because you are both my relatives. Although I would like to be on the side of truth I don't want to be against you, Duryodhana. I would rather not participate in this war at all. If I have to participate, then I will not kill anybody or even touch a weapon, so I will be useless. But I have a big army of strong warriors. One of you can have my army and the other can have me. Because I saw Arjuna first and because he is younger I am going to let him choose. The eldest brother must have patience and the youngest has the right to ask first. Now, Arjuna, tell me what you want: me without my army and with a vow not to fight or my army with all its warriors and weapons."

Out of love Arjuna sometimes addressed Krishna as Madhura (the one who is enchanting for everybody). He said, "Madhura, I don't need your army, it can join Duryodhana. I only want you because you are on the side of truth and victory is always with truth.* I would like you to be my charioteer."

Duryodhana said to himself, "What a fool; he could have had Krishna's army. I feared that I would get the useless son of a cowboy. God must be on my side, wanting me to win. I got what I wanted."

So when Krishna asked Duryodhana's opinion he said, "I honor my stupid brother and I gladly accept your offer. You can be on the side of Arjuna if you will not fight. For you to be neutral is good. I prefer to make use of your army."

———◆———

This incident illustrates Arjuna's character. Most people would choose quantity, but Arjuna went after quality. A warrior depended on his chariot and his charioteer very much. Having a good charioteer who understood war and knew when to move forward and when to escape was a great help for a warrior. As he was a devotee of Krishna, nothing

---

*In India on every currency note it is written, "Ultimately truth wins." Similarly, on American currency it is written, "In God we trust." They don't, but they say it.

was more valuable for him than having Krishna on his side. Arjuna was egoless most of the time. That might be one of the causes of the successes in his life. He wasn't a saint; he was a man with human weaknesses, but they were compensated for by his devotion.

Trimming the Ego

Sometimes it is good to think in terms of "I," the ahamkara, the ego. But when we get too full of our own ego and all the time have that big "I," and say, "I don't know" and, "I don't believe in it," then we become isolated. Once, as a young poet, I met a very good poet who said, "Nobody knows how to write poems except me and you."

I said, "Then I am the only one who knows everything because you know nothing." When I used the same tool on him that he was using on everybody else he was sad that he had talked like that.

The thing is that each of us has a picture of himself or herself as covering the whole universe. That is the cover of ego. Only humility and friendship can trim it down. Friendship with god is the highest kind of relationship that anybody can have. But most people do not feel competent enough to be friendly with god. They feel like they have so many problems inside that they cannot get close to god. But *bhakti* (devotion) teaches you how to play with god.

Karna Gives His Armor to Indra

When war was imminent Indra started fearing that the life of his son Arjuna was endangered by his greatest enemy, Karna. As the son of the sun god, Karna was born with a natural breastplate and earrings that made him practically invincible. The breastplate protected him against all kinds of weapons. The earrings were radiant like the sun and as long as they were in his ears nobody could harm him.

Karna was doing a sadhana of charity, thus earning good karma in order to get an opportunity to kill his opponent Arjuna. He would distribute fruit and wealth to brahmins. He had sworn to give anything within his means to a brahmin begging for anything at his door after he finished his puja.

Indra decided to weaken Karna by taking advantage of his vow. He disguised himself as a brahmin. While he was on his way, Surya found out that Indra was planning to cheat Karna and decided to warn him. When Karna was doing his mantra for the sun god, Surya descended from his chariot right in front of Karna. He told him, "My son, I am your father, the sun god. I have come to warn you that Indra is on his way to you. I cannot stop him but don't let him cheat you. Don't give him what he wants." Then Surya left again.

When Karna had just finished his puja Indra came knocking on Karna's door disguised as a brahmin asking for alms. Karna pretended that he didn't know who the brahmin was and he played his role. Traditionally any visiting brahmin should be honored. He should be offered a seat, food and drink, and even a footwashing. So Karna called the brahmin in, offered him a nice place to sit, nice food and drinks, and said, "Please sit down. I am bringing all that I have and I will give it to you."

Indra said, "I am not a brahmin. I am Indra and you know it because you have been told. I am not here for this. I am not coming to take any wealth from you. I need something important that you have and you have to give it to me. I want your armor and your earrings."

Karna hesitated, "They are my protection given to me by my father. When I fight with Arjuna, I will need them. But you have come at the time when I cannot refuse anybody anything. If you could compensate my loss somehow then I would be more willing to give them to you."

Indra showed his Shakti astra to Karna saying, "This missile is charged with my energy. It is guaranteed to kill any enemy, but only one. If you hit Arjuna with it he will certainly be killed. After that the energy will return to me and the weapon will not work anymore, so you'd better think twice before you use it."

Karna tore the armor off his breast, cut the rings from his ears, and gave them to Indra. He accepted the weapon in return and thought he was well *equipped to defeat Arjuna. He didn't realize how handicapped he was without his protection.*

———————◆———————

Karna Meets His Mother

Karna had always known that the lady who had fostered him was not his real mother. He had been given shelter by the charioteer of the king, so naturally he belonged to the side of Dhritarashtra. Because he was not a member of the warrior class, he was repressed by Bhishma and Drona and other members of the royal family. They put him down constantly.

Repeatedly telling a person he is wrong even if he tries his best is the easiest way to stop him from growing and make him feel he is not right. It increased Karna's jealousy and resentment against Arjuna. He became friends with Duryodhana who needed him to oppose Arjuna, as they were equally skilled in archery. So Karna became an enemy of his own brothers because Kunti never told him that he was her son. But that was not the only reason for Karna to hate Arjuna. They had to become enemies because Karna was an incarnation of the demon Sahasrabahu, who finally had to be defeated by Arjuna and Krishna.

When the war became imminent Krishna tried to prevent it by telling Karna that he was a son of Kunti and that he should not fight his own brother. But Karna replied, "Telling me the truth has harmed me more than not knowing the truth. It was the main purpose of my life to kill Arjuna. I would have fought him with all my might and been satisfied to defeat him. Knowing that he is my younger brother weakens my moral strength. You have destroyed the purpose of my life, which is the greatest offense anybody can do. But even then I will fight and do my dharma as I should."

Right before the start of the war Kunti went to Karna to talk with him and she told him she was his mother. Karna was glad to finally meet his mother, but he also felt pain. He said, "You should have told me this before when I challenged Arjuna and when Drona and Kripa did not let me compete with him."

Kunti said, "I am sorry, but I cannot change the past. Why don't you leave Duryodhana and join our side?"

Karna knew Duryodhana was not right and actually he was against Duryodhana at every move, but still nobody could persuade him to get away from Duryodhana. He said, "I am bound to do my duty. Duryodhana trusts me and I will not break his trust. I refuse to fight against him. Better for me is to die the way I am and remain loyal to the one who has been kind to me. It is not that I want to serve evil people, but only they gave me shelter when I was rejected by society as an illegal child. Only the mafia helped me to grow up and gave meaning to my life. Should I leave them and join the normal society? What do you think?"

Kunti agreed, "Yes, if you are a follower of truth you should leave them. But if you cannot leave Duryodhana then at least promise me you will not kill your brothers."

Karna said, "I can promise that I will not kill Yudhishthira, Bhima, Nakula, or Sahadeva, but Arjuna I will kill. You are famous for having five sons and you will always have five sons.* If Arjuna dies, then with me you will have five sons. And if I die, then with Arjuna you have five sons. So there will be no loss for you."

Duryodhana Tricks Shalya

In his efforts to gather an army twice as big as that of his enemies, Duryodhana discovered that Madrunaresh Shalya, brother of Madri and maternal uncle of Nakula and Sahadeva, was on his way with his army to join the Pandavas. When evening was falling, courtiers of Duryodhana came to King Shalya and

---

*Kunti had adopted Nakula and Sahadeva.

said, "Our king has sent us to help you set up your camp. We have already made tents and prepared some food for you. Please come."

When Shalya asked who had sent them they said it was his nephew. He thought they meant Yudhishthira. But, as Yudhishthira's cousin brother, Duryodhana in a way was also a nephew of Shalya. At every place where King Shalya and his army halted, they received good treatment, food, and all kinds of facilities. He was delighted, thinking, "My nephews are so good, they have arranged so much so well. I must help them." When he asked, "Where are my nephews? I want to see them," he was told, "They are coming."

When Duryodhana entered the camp, Shalya recognized the man he had come all the way from Madradesh to fight against. Shalya was amazed and asked, "You are here?"

Duryodhana said, "I have been taking care of you. All the places where you have rested have been arranged by my people."

The uncle said, "Yes, but I wanted to go to Yudhishthira."

Duryodhana said, "Sure, you wanted to go to Yudhishthira and you can still go. We will not stop you, we only tried to give you a good feeling because you are also our uncle."

Now the uncle was morally disturbed. He had been eating food from Duryodhana and using the places provided by him for some days. He said, "I will inform my army that I will stay with you and help you."

Duryodhana said, "No, we don't need your army. We were just serving you selflessly. You can go and join your nephews."

But Shalya's army said, "Sir, we have been eating their salt. Now we have to be true to the salt and we cannot fight against them. We should join them."

Shalya said, "Duryodhana, you have tricked me. Now I cannot go and help my nephews. I will be on your side." But inside he felt it was wrong.

———◆———

The Laws of War

It had been decided that there would be war. Both sides had gathered their armies and each side had chosen a commander in chief. Bhishma was commander of the Kaurava army and Dhrishtadyumna commanded the Pandava forces. In Dvapara Yuga wars were more a matter of duty than of hate. The enemy was fought not because of hate but rather because of principle and ego problems. In the evening before the start of the war both commanders in chief came together and agreed on the laws of war that had to be respected.

The first law was that the fighting would be between sunrise and sunset and that there would be no attacks at night. After sunset the warriors would be recovering from the injuries of the day. Visitors were allowed to enter the opposing camp and give medical care to wounded relatives. Nowadays towns are bombarded at night while people are asleep, but in the old days that was against the law.

The second law was that one man would fight with one man only. If two were fighting then others could watch, but they were not allowed to interfere except if one lost his weapon; then a friend could give him another weapon to continue the fight.

The third law was that only equals should fight. In those days battles were always fought far away from cities and civilians. People who were old or sick, women and children were never attacked. An infantry soldier would only fight with another soldier on foot; a warrior with an elephant would only fight another warrior with an elephant. If you were much stronger than your opponent you had to warn him and show your power to scare him off. Only if he remained could you kill him. If anybody lost his weapon he was allowed to pick up another one. Similarly in some old Western movies a cowboy gives a gun to an unarmed opponent and then challenges him to fight. That is true bravery. Warriors always fought man-to-man duels at arm's length distance or within reach of arrows, but always within sight. The arrival of gunpowder changed warfare completely all over the world. Suddenly warriors had the power to strike from a distance without being seen. This made wars more destructive and cruel. Nowadays people are killed by cheating and crimes. Several countries can combine their military and technical power against a small country. They create havoc and destroy all resources by carpet bombing, and then make a contract to rebuild the country for billions of dollars.

⟨Ỿ⟩

Gandhari Blesses the Pandavas

Gandhari was selfless in character; she loved the Pandavas as much as she loved her own children. She told Duryodhana not to indulge in his power game, but it was useless. She knew the truth and accepted it. She knew her son was evil, so instead of blessing him she blessed the Pandavas, "May you be victorious over the evil."

That annoyed Duryodhana and he said, "You are my mother, but you bless my enemies by wishing them victory over me."

She replied, "The truth is that those who are on the right path will be victorious anyway and you are not, so you will suffer. Today you may enjoy wealth and power, but soon this kingdom will be without you."

———◆———

PART THREE

❧

The Bhagavad Gita

18
Arjuna Refuses to Fight

Everything was prepared to start the war. The two armies had moved to the huge plain of Kurukshetra. Scouts had informed all the kings and commanders and they had described the opponents' chariots, flags, and horses and summed up their fathers and forefathers. One row of Pandavas was standing opposite one row of Kauravas and they could see each other.

Krishna Gives Arjuna a Lesson in Karma Yoga

Arjuna asked Krishna to drive his chariot to the middle of the battlefield from where he could see all the great heroes. He wanted to see his grandfather, teacher, uncles, cousins, and nephews. Many would be dead tomorrow. Everybody watched the chariot moving to the middle of the battlefield. The situation was highly unusual. According to tradition the commanders in chief of both sides, Dhrishtadyumna and Bhishma, had to blow their conches to signal the start of the war. Before that nobody would make a move.

Duryodhana was puzzled. Maybe Arjuna had become fearful, seeing such a big army, and now he wanted to make a compromise to avoid war. He asked Drona and Bhishma what was the matter, but they did not know either. King Dhritarashtra wanted to know what was happening, but he could *not see the battlefield. His charioteer Sanjay had to describe the situation to him. Sanjay was just an ordinary chariot driver, but Vyasa had given him the divine power to see beyond the horizon and to see the story behind the story. He closed his eyes, used his divine sight, and then told the king what was happening.* King Dhritarashtra listened with full attention. He had good hopes that the war would not start and that his sons would be saved, but it did not happen that way.*

Arjuna took a look at his relatives and all the others. He felt that he cared about them and the idea of killing them disgusted him. He threw down his bow and arrows and sat down on the ground in the middle of the battlefield. He said to Krishna, "If I have to kill these people to get my kingdom, I refuse to fight. It is better to have no kingdom than to kill the people that are so close. Bhishma is like a grandfather to me. In my childhood I played in his lap. When I had pain he consoled me, and when I was sick he took care of me all night. Drona taught me all that I know and I adore him. I shared my childhood with my cousins and we grew up together. I care about these people and now only for a small kingdom should I kill them? Tell me if that body that I call 'my grandfather' is actually only a body or is there a spirit inside that is my grandfather?"

Krishna said, "Yes there is a spirit inside, but it is nobody's grandfather and nobody's enemy. In this theater he happens to be your grandfather and you happen to be his grandson. But in fact neither is he your grandfather nor are you his grandson."

Arjuna said, "If this world is merely a theater for our spirits and if our bodies are only costumes to wear during the play, then this kingdom seems false and not worth fighting for."

Krishna said, "You are right. From times immemorial people came and claimed this land. They all died and their ashes got mixed with the soil. In fact this land belongs to nobody. But at the moment you should not fight to get your land but to defend your rights, which is something else. Don't allow bad people to deprive you and your brothers of your belongings. The scriptures say that you have to protect your rights."

---

*The Mahabharata describes the war through Sanjay's voice.

Krishna said, "Apart from denying you the kingdom the Kauravas have done you much wrong. Duryodhana tried to poison and to burn your family. Dushasana pulled Draupadi into the courtroom and tried to undress her and nobody protested. When Duryodhana told Draupadi to sit on his lap, Bhima swore an oath to break Duryodhana's thigh and you swore an oath to shoot him as soon as you were free. If you are an honorable man, then you have to stick to your word and fight."

When Arjuna had been preparing for war he had constantly remembered the problems that had been caused by Duryodhana and they inspired him to fight, but that day the inspiration had vanished. He forgot the enmity of his vow because he was caught by emotion and attachment, which are two human weaknesses that create many problems. When evil is caused by a relative, a friend, or personal weakness, we feel related to the evil doer and it becomes difficult to fight the evil.

In spite of all the wrong the Kauravas had done to him, Arjuna cared about them. He said, "Maybe at one time they have been bad. They really insulted my wife and put me down, but that is not such a crime that I should kill them. Time has passed and now I don't feel as bad about it as I did before. It feels wrong to kill them. I would rather live like a beggar in a place where nobody knows me than to fight against my own people."

Krishna said, "You may talk like a wise man, but you are not fully aware of what you are saying. Your words are only a shield to hide your weakness. Your feelings of family and affection are only lame excuses to avoid doing your dharma and fulfilling your karma. You refuse to fight because you have a mental disease called attachment. When an earthquake happens you want your relatives and friends to be spared because of your personal attachments, but everybody becomes the victim of the same disaster. Likewise in a war nobody is spared. At the moment attachment is your greatest problem and it is clouding your view.

"If you consider your conflict with Duryodhana as something personal then you can choose not to fight. But then you promote evil like these people

did when they allowed Draupadi to be pulled into the court. You have to fight them to teach them a lesson; otherwise you allow them to mistreat other women as well. If you refuse to fight injustice and leave it to others, then you defeat yourself and the purpose of your life. A society that tolerates injustice has to perish."

Krishna continued, "Do you think I don't know that fighting is bad? Nothing is more disastrous than war. War cannot be justified, even if it is a crusade for religion. But I tried my best to maintain peace. I went to the Kauravas with a peace proposal, but Duryodhana refused to give even a small piece of land. Then war became unavoidable.

"We gathered our armies and selected our commander in chief and we agreed upon the laws of war. Now that everything has been prepared, you refuse to fight. You are like a coward who runs away from his duty. You are a warrior and it is said that when a warrior dies of sickness in his bed he goes to hell, but when he dies on the battlefield he attains the highest merit. So as a warrior you must reach for the highest merit and fight. In your life your action is not guided by what you would like to do but by the circumstances in which you are placed. Now we are on the battlefield and it is too late to discuss the pros and cons of war."

Arjuna said, "Now either explain my duty or turn the chariot back and leave the battlefield. It is not worthwhile for the sake of name and fame to kill these people who did many great deeds. It is better to be called a coward who lost everything and is defeated. I will not fight."

Krishna said, "With a clear perspective you will see that Duryodhana and his people are on the side of injustice. Duryodhana always tortures and destroys people. He cannot be a subject matter of pity; he should be punished for his injustice. The people who support him accept the injustice, so they are a party to it and should be punished as well. You have to save the world from the dominance of wrong people."

Arjuna replied, "It is true that the world is filled with bad elements. But I am too small and the world is too big. I cannot change the world and I cannot do anything."

Krishna said, "It is true you cannot do anything. But actually who are you?

You are just a manifestation of man, but the energy inside you is eternal. It was never born and it will never die. It is without beginning and without end. The body will be destroyed, but the spirit is beyond destruction. So why should you worry? You should do your dharma. A warrior has to fight injustice even though victory is not in his hands because at any moment invisible factors can bring defeat. Do your duty without thinking about results and leave the rest in the hands of god and you will be free."

It is difficult to inspire somebody to fight because fighting is bad. But Krishna explained to Arjuna that good and bad are intermingled. He explained the important point that we are confused about our identity, which makes it difficult for us to see things in a real perspective and causes all kinds of problems. He gave him a lesson in karma yoga. He explained that he had to fight in order to follow his dharma and fulfill his karma.

The dialogue between Krishna and Arjuna is the most important part of the Mahabharata. It is available everywhere as a small separate book called Srimad Bhagavad Gita. It concentrates on our ego-attachments to people with whom we relate like mother, brother, uncle, or beloved. It pertains to every human being because the fight between the Kauravas and Pandavas also represents the war between the vices and virtues in all of us.

Inner Dynamics

The whole game of a human being goes on between body, mind, intellect, ego, and Self (*atman*). Body, mind, intellect, and ego belong to nature (*prakriti*) but the Self is beyond that. It is a spark of the divine.

When the Self accepts the role of an individual being, it needs operational consciousness to guide the being, to possess the body, and to work with it. That is the job of ego, mind, and intellect. Ego is the one that possesses everything, intellect is the guiding consciousness, and mind is the one that goes everywhere to find things. When ego wants to enjoy something, mind finds out how to get it, and if necessary intellect consults all the available knowledge. Mind, intellect, ego, and Self move from one body to the next until the fascination for life is completely gone and the person is purified. Then the individual consciousness is ready to merge into the cosmic consciousness.

Ego and mind are the main actors in the game of life. Mind and matter are two sides of the same coin; mind makes matter alive. Intellect has the information from the past and present; on the basis of that it extrapolates the present situation to the future. It is the intellect that the scriptures speak to. The inner voice of your intellect tells you whether something you are doing is right or wrong. But often when the intellect says that something is wrong and will cause suffering, the ego decides to do it anyway. Many times in your life you overrule the inner voice because you like what you are doing.

We always forget that we are consciousness and we identify with our ego, which is ignorance or illusion (*maya*). If we can get away from this illusion then there is no more pain and no more suffering. All the pain and suffering of life is a result of hanging on to the illusion of ego. Taking illusions to be real creates the problems. If we understand the truth then all problems are gone. The truth is only one: there is only one spirit in which everything exists. Nothing happens outside of that. Everything happens inside the supreme being or god. He is bigger, stronger, more intelligent; he can take care of himself. You have to only do your role.

Attachment to the Body

Because ego identifies with the body we get too attached to the body. When I was a boy I asked my father, "Can I feel you?" He said, "Okay touch me." But when I touched him he said, "You are touching my hand, not me." I kept on searching, but everywhere I touched it was a part of his body but not really him. Then I understood that actually my father is someone inside the body whom I cannot touch. If we could understand that then we could detach from our body, but we always confuse our body with our self.

Ego thinks "I am the body and I am getting old and weak," but ego never wants to die. When I was sixteen years old I thought, "I can die when I am twenty-eight." When I was twenty-eight I thought, "Let me have some more years until I am thirty-five." When I was thirty-five I said to myself, "I want to see my little children grow up. Wait until I am seventy-five." But when I am seventy-five I will say, "Let me live for twenty-five more years to complete a hundred years." Human nature is not satisfied with living for a hundred or even five hundred years, so in fact everybody wants to be immortal. But the body cannot be immortal because everything that has been created also has to be destroyed. Each minute there are cells in the body dying. And when death takes away lots of pains it is a great relief.

People hardly think about life and death. Every day death is around us and we go to funerals and crematoriums, but we think of the death of other people only. When somebody is ill or when somebody dear dies we think about life and death for a few minutes and then we quickly return to fantasies, attachments, and life. After a few minutes we forget that we are mortal even if we are reminded a thousand times a day. If we were more conscious about our own death then there would be less attachment to all the things that will be left behind when we expire.

Some people confuse themselves with their car and think they are distinguished if their car is costly and special. But we should consider our body as a rented car and think, "I have only rented this car so it does not belong to me. I rented it because I have to cover some distance. I should drive it carefully and have a nice journey, but I should not get attached to it. And when my journey is over I will give it back." People who realize that they are more than body and body consciousness don't think death is real and don't fear death. On the game board of the *Leela** book all of the stages of life are there, but there is no death

---

The Yoga of Snakes and Arrows: The Leela of Self-Knowledge (Rochester, Vt.: Destiny Books, 2007).

in it because death is not real. The truth is that one never dies because consciousness never dies.

∘⭗∘

Krishna Reminds Arjuna of His Duty to Fight Injustice

Arjuna had been born in a lineage of warriors who were supposed to protect the truth and oppose untruth, injustice, and cruelty. Krishna said, "You were born as a son of Kunti and a member of the clan of Bharata. But is this your true identity? Are you really a son of Kunti and a member of the clan of Bharata or are you more than that?"

Arjuna said, "I am a son of Kunti and I am related to these people because they are members of the clan of Bharata, as I am. Otherwise I am pure consciousness, but at the moment that consciousness is colored by the situation."

Krishna replied, "Then as a warrior, as a member of the royal family, and as a member of the clan of Bharata, it is your duty to see that there is justice, honesty, and peace in the kingdom. But the whole country is suffering because of the dishonesty and selfishness of the Kauravas. Therefore you have to punish injustice and fight."

Arjuna said, "There you have a point, but my mind is confused, my eyes don't see, my hands don't want to hold the arrow, and I don't want to fight my own people."

———◆———

Arjuna was taken away by his attachment to his body. He had forgotten that his true identity was consciousness and that the body is only a tool. By mistake he was identifying himself with the person as whom he was born. That false identification made him run away from his duty. Just as he identified himself with his body, he identified his opponents with their bodies. In each person he saw a relationship to which he felt attached. But this life is only one particular expression of consciousness. Consciousness is life after life and it is related to nobody. Thus the fact that Arjuna's opponents were his relatives was not a valid excuse for not doing his duty.

19

Fighting for Justice and Truth

At the end of the Dvapara Yuga lots of evil entered the human psychodrama and the law of dharma was violated in many ways. People were not honest anymore; they had become demagogues. Outside they appeared to be great brahmins and people who knew dharma, but inside they were just supporting the doers of evil because they got their bread and butter through them. Powerful people were only interested in their own power and not in the welfare of humanity at large.

When Draupadi was brought to the court of Dhritarashtra and harassed, everybody just watched and she had to take care of herself; Krishna was the only one who helped her. Vidura was the only one who stood up and left the hall. Bhishma, Drona, and Kripa knew that something wrong was happening, but they swallowed their anger because they were on the payroll of Duryodhana's father and they had to honor the king. They were sitting there and they let it happen; they did not even say, "Shame, shame." By remaining silent they all became party to the insult of Draupadi. If they had opposed Duryodhana then he would not have had the courage to drag Draupadi into the court. Supporting the evil Duryodhana made them also evil.

It is said that silence is half acceptance. When I do something and you remain silent I understand that you agree; only when you protest do I know that you don't agree. When something wrong happens in your presence and you do not protest, then you are not fulfilling the purpose of your life. If you don't understand that it is wrong then you are ignorant and you are also not fulfilling the purpose of your life.

Because of our attachment to our body we grant favors to our weaknesses. We play all kinds of games to satisfy our eyes, ears, nose, tongue, and skin with touch, taste, sound, and visuals. Just to satisfy our senses we allow wrong things to happen to our own body, our natural environment, and our society. All relations between people are maintained by ego and body. Therefore, just as we grant favors to our weaknesses because of our attachment to our body, we also grant favors to our relatives and friends. If my cousin does something wrong and I close my eyes because it is my cousin, then I allow the wrong thing to happen and that wrong thing will create more wrong things and a whole network of wrong things starts floating around. If my cousin and somebody else do something wrong and I spare my cousin but punish the other, then the other will blame me for being partial.

In the eyes of justice everybody should be equal and there should be no prejudice and no favors. Justice does not discriminate between wife and husband, father and son, family and others. That's why they depict justice as blind. A mother should always be just and honest and not excuse her child because it is her child. There are stories about mothers that did not tolerate injustice and punished or even killed their sons for the sake of saving the weak, the poor, and the helpless.

When a society becomes bad, individuals become important, nobody has authority any longer, and injustice increases. To get justice in a rotten society people have to pay lawyers, go to court, and waste their time and money. But when people lose the understanding of right and wrong, then even a court order and a police force cannot establish justice. For that people have to restore their understanding of right and wrong. Once a society has become so corrupted that people witness evil and lack the courage to oppose it, then that society has to give way to a healthy one where people can be trusted. The kingdom should be ruled by people who care for truth and justice, who support human rights, who let good people flourish, and who respect women. Respect for each other is a common principle: your liberty ends where my nose begins. If you want your rights then you also have to be conscious of the rights of others.

In a living society people gather around something wrong happening and they stop it themselves. In third-world countries even today, if injustice is done to somebody on the street, then people who are passing by will stop and interfere. But in big towns like Delhi and Bombay somebody can get murdered in broad daylight and people passing by will avoid the place where it is happening because they have no time to answer questions from the police and to testify in court. Recently a boy whom I know went to France and right in the railway station in Paris he was robbed at the point of a knife. Hundreds of people were present on the platform and saw four guys bugging one young person, but nobody came to help. In the time of the Mahabharata the situation was similar.

If somebody comes and takes away my glass of water it could be the start of a war. But a problem between two people is a personal affair and not a right cause of war. But if somebody deprives a whole community of water then it is a social problem, which is a right cause of war. To decide what is right and wrong you should see all sides as a neutral person. Vyasa was kind not to write a different Mahabharata in which Draupadi jumps into the battlefield before the conch blows to kill the man who had pulled her hair and dragged her to the court. It would not have been justified to kill out of that kind of anger. If Arjuna had fought for personal reasons like getting the kingdom or taking revenge for the insult to Draupadi, then his cause would not have been just. But it was justified to fight a society that tolerated injustice and tortured women. He had to be neutral and fight for justice, not for taking revenge. It was his duty to help his brothers to restore the understanding of right and wrong.

Truth Never Changes

Reality may appear real and objective to you, but it is subjective. Two people may both be looking at me, but each will be getting a different impression; the image of me in each will be different. When I say, "I love you" it is only true for this moment (relative truth) because tomorrow you might do me wrong and I would start hating you. Since I do not know what will happen I cannot say I will do something and be absolutely sure that I will really do it.

Truth is never changing and whatever never changes is truth (absolute truth). Changing things are not true; they are illusions that cannot be trusted. Sixty years ago I was a small baby inside the body of my mother. Since then I have changed in many ways, but which one is the real me? The truth is that the body is not the truth. Something that is constantly changing cannot be real. All objects in this world are constantly changing. Today they are like this and tomorrow like that. The world of names and forms is illusion. Similarly the warriors in the battlefield of Kurukshetra were illusion.

We forget eternal values and run after temporary values. We collect garbage inside and outside, but coming generations will throw away the garbage from their ancestors and buy new plastic garbage. Some day we may realize that by depending upon changing things, by trusting them, by loving them and thinking about them, we are only wasting time and energy. In this everchanging world, how can we take anything to be permanent and get seriously emotionally involved? Why unnecessarily waste our energy on thinking about something temporary? Why not think about something permanent like truth, justice, and humanity, which are needed as long as humankind survives? Nowadays there is no Arjuna, but truth, justice, and humanity are still required. These concepts are primary; they are beyond time and space and they should be supported. And personal attachment and personal values should be brought to the background.

Problems of Short-term Thinking

Today a bell is ringing to tell us that our future is in danger because of increasing pollution, but we are sitting silent without opposing it. Once in a while somebody makes a signature campaign or a march at night with torches. But these games are mostly organized to gain popularity and nobody actually challenges what is happening. In periods of crisis and injustice our role is not to sit down and just watch; we must act. One individual cannot do much, but a group can make many other people conscious of what is happening and they can fight the battle. Just as in the Mahabharata, we need warriors like Arjuna and his brothers and a wise person like Krishna to fight the battle. Wisdom points to the right way, but it does not destroy the evil. For destruction of evil the action of Arjuna is needed.

There are people who are doing it, but they are political, like in the green party. They are trying to become more environmentally friendly and educate others, but when they get the power they do the same things as the others who don't talk about ecology. Most people who are working in this direction are doing it with political motives to become more popular and nobody is sincere. If people honestly think that this pollution is wrong then it will change, but everybody is too busy in their own world. As long as the crisis is tolerable nothing happens. But the day will come when things will get so bad that our bodies will face many problems just to survive. Then maybe a new Arjuna and Krishna will be born to change this completely. We should be conscious that we are destroying our environment by short-term planning of just ten or a hundred years and not considering the long-term effects of what we are doing. Time-bound consciousness and death are the things that prevent human beings from thinking in a broader perspective; that creates problems for life. We are taking all the great treasures out of Mother Earth and emptying her body, thinking, "Nature is unkind and makes me suffer. I must conquer nature to create luxury for myself." We did not think about being friendly to our environment.

Today the problems have grown and we have started having conferences and seminars about ecology. When I first went to America in 1969 there was a famous poet called Gary Snyder who used to talk about ecology. At first I thought he was crazy because I thought, "Earth is very big; three quarters of it is water and only one quarter is land and on that quarter people are only living in a narrow belt. So they can only destroy a small amount and there is no danger for Earth." But I changed my mind when I studied the descriptions of the damage that is being done.

Just as I could not believe that the environment was seriously damaged, you cannot believe the story of Mahabharata and that life is a continuum of consciousness. Look at the tea in this cup. If you pour it out the water will evaporate, enter the atmosphere, reach the clouds, and become liquid again. Similarly, when consciousness is in your body it may be impure and ignorant. But when your body is finished, it becomes pure consciousness again. And as long as desires remain, the cycle of birth and death continues, and consciousness will incarnate again.

20

Krishna Shows Arjuna His Glorious Shape

Arjuna is individual consciousness (human) and Krishna is cosmic consciousness (god). They are two aspects of the same consciousness. Arjuna only can see as much as his limited senses permit, but Krishna sees the truth objectively and everything from beginning to end. When Arjuna was confused by genetic information, attachments, relationships, and emotions, he found it difficult to decide upon his course of action. Krishna, who is beyond relationships and emotions, resolved Arjuna's confusion by reminding him of his original form, like in the story of the cub and the lion.

The Cub and the Lion

Once a shepherd was herding his sheep when he found a small lion cub in the forest. He brought the cub home and kept it with his sheep. He gave it food and all it needed so that it was growing well. When the shepherd went to the forest with his sheep he used to take the cub with him on a chain. One day while he was grazing the sheep and playing his flute a big lion came from the jungle and made a terrible roaring sound. All the sheep were terrified and fled away and so did the shepherd, but the lion cub remained standing at the same spot.

The big lion approached him and asked, "Why are you still here when all your company has run away?"

The cub replied, "Because your sound does not scare me."

The big lion said, "There is a reason for that. Come with me, I will show you." The big lion took the cub to a pool of water and said, "Look at your face in the water and then look at my face."

The cub saw that his face very much resembled the face of the big lion and said, "Hey, we look alike!"

The big lion said, "Yes, we are the same and that is why you were not afraid of my sound and did not run away. We are hunters, but the others are sheep who only eat plants."

The cub said, "That is cool."

The big lion said, "Yes, you can have fun with that. Go back to those sheep and make the sound that I taught you. Then all of them, including your master, will run away, and you will feel great."

The lion cub went back to the shepherd and the sheep and they all saw him coming back. They surrounded him and said, "What happened? Why didn't you run away with us? We were waiting for you and we were worried you might be injured by the big lion."

He said, "No, I am not afraid," and then he looked at everybody and made a roaring sound. All the sheep and the shepherd ran away. The lion cub felt free because he was not a pet of the shepherd anymore but an independent lion.

———◆———

This story from the Upanishads tells you that the lion cub (individual consciousness / Arjuna) and the big lion from the jungle (consciousness in its original form / Krishna) are basically the same. The cub had become a pet in the hands of a shepherd. But when the cub understood that he was a lion rather than a sheep he became a free lion that roams around in the jungle.

Another story of Krishna makes the same point in a different way.

◦◆◦

The Brahmin's Wife

One day the gopis were sitting with Krishna. It was already after midnight and Krishna wanted them to go home and get some sleep because otherwise they would be tired the next morning. But as usual the gopis didn't want to leave. Time and again Krishna asked them to go home, but they would not move. Krishna got annoyed and said, "Why don't you go home? Your people at home will be worried. Go home!"

They said, "If you answer our question we will go home."

Krishna said, "Okay, what is the question?"

They said, "We need to introduce it with a small story." Krishna agreed.

The gopis said, "Once upon a time there was a brahmin. He had a wife and they loved each other very much. One day the brahmin got a command from the king to go abroad for several months for an important job. He told his wife, 'I'm going away for some months on a government job. I know it will be too much for you to be alone and you will feel sad.' So he brought a picture of himself and said, 'Here is a picture of me. Keep it in front of you and remember me whenever you miss me. I will come back as soon as possible.'

"The lady was happy that when her husband was gone at least she could look at the picture of him. The next day she went to the framer to get the picture framed and she put it in her shrine. Every day when she was doing her work she meditated on her husband's picture and tried to communicate mentally with him. One day while she was doing her worship somebody knocked at the door. She did not hear it because she was deep in meditation.

"Then the person shouted, 'Open the door.' She recognized the voice of her husband. He had come back from abroad and wanted to enter the house, but the door was locked from the inside.

"Now the question is: should she keep on worshipping the picture and complete her meditation or should she get up and open the door for her husband? What do you think?"

Krishna said, "I think she should get up and open the door."

The gopis said, "That is the problem. All this universe is a picture of you.

Every man is a picture of you, but you are the real person. Now we are with the real husband and you ask us to go and worship a picture. How can we leave you to go home and be with your picture?"

Krishna had no answer.

We should understand that we are so attached to maya that we keep on worshipping a picture of god all our life; we don't want to open the door for the original god who is knocking on our door.

> ### Calming the Mind
>
> The mind is confused by *maya*, the world of names and forms, emotions, reasons, and attachments; therefore it cannot rest. For that restless mind an infinite form is required to calm it by show-ing the mind that it is so small. To give the mind an infinite form we cannot produce a form of the one who has no form and we cannot make finite the one who is infinite. But we can give the formless so many forms that we create an idea of infinity. Each of us can add our image of god to all the other images of the same god. (But people also separate their gods and sometimes even god separates himself, saying, "Thou shall not worship any other god.")

In the Bhagavad Gita, Krishna calms Arjuna with the aid of a vision.

Krishna Reveals His Glorious Shape

Krishna said, "Dharma should be followed without any reasoning and without any exception. You must do your duty. A warrior has the duty to fight and to protect justice."

Arjuna still did not understand it because his body was disturbed by emotions. The prospect of killing his grandfather, his teacher, and the other great people made him sad and he could not accept it. Krishna wanted him to understand that though all the warriors looked real they were not. He said, "At the moment you are taken away by emotions. You have forgotten your knowledge and are judging the entire situation from a limited point of view. You and I both have taken birth many times. The difference between us is that you do not remember your past lives whereas I remember them all. All that exists is only atman. Everything comes out from god and goes back to god. So in fact all the warriors here are nobody but the same god in different forms. It is his game that god is killing god. He likes it this way. Who are you to prevent it from happening?"

Then Krishna said, "I have explained enough. Now you should see." He expanded himself and the whole universe was covered by his presence. The battlefield and all the warriors in front of Arjuna's eyes disappeared and all around he only saw only Krishna. From one side all human beings, animals, plants, and minerals were moving in a queue toward Krishna, merging into Krishna, and nothing remained. Then, on the other side, everything was coming out of Krishna again. On one side life was starting and on the other side it was ending, and in between was the whole universe.*

Arjuna could not behold this vision and he said, "I am getting confused and afraid because you are so huge. I am too small to conceive such a gigantic form. When god is in human form I can associate with him as I can associate with a human being. Please come back to your normal form and then I will follow your advice."

Then Krishna adopted his human form again. Arjuna felt comfortable and said, "Now I have seen that all that exists is only you. Everything comes from you and goes back to you. Nobody is actually killing anybody. All happens inside you. In that case I don't feel that I am doing anything wrong. Now I am ready to fight."

Krishna moved the chariot back to the Pandava army.

———◆———

*See the frontispiece painting *Kurukshetra* by Prabhat Bal.

PART FOUR

❦

War and Its Aftermath

21

The Start of the War

On the deathbed of his father, Bhishma had promised to take care of the kingdom of Hastinapura and to support the one on the throne as much as he had supported the dying King Shantanu. Because of that promise he was bound to Duryodhana and he served the evil side all his life. He knew that Duryodhana was evil, but he could not join the Pandavas. As a grandfather, as a warrior, and as a counselor he told Duryodhana that he was wrong. But then Duryodhana would say, "Listen, I am the king. You shut up." And then Bhishma would obey and did not rebel. That is a weakness in human character. All over the world things are hidden because we don't speak out, like the abused wife who thinks, "How can I tell anybody what my husband is doing?" That creates problems later.

Bhishma had no personal interest in the war; it was only for the sake of the country that he became the commander in chief of the Kaurava army. It was a misfortune that a follower of dharma had to fight against good guys like Krishna and Arjuna. Riding a white chariot with white horses and a white flag, he was surrounded by impure people who were only guided by the lower chakras. He was involved only because he was not flexible and did not interpret dharma in his own way, expanding its meaning to make it more valid. Because he could not change his mind he was caught by his commitment.

❦

The War Begins

When both armies were ready to start fighting, Yudhishthira got down from his chariot, walked to the other side of the battlefield to Bhishma, touched his feet, and said, "Grandfather, now we are in the battlefield as enemies. I have to fight you because it is my dharma. You know that you are on the side of wrong people, but you are bound by your vow to protect the throne of Hastinapura. Although I have to fight you, please give me your blessings."

Bhishma said, "You will be victorious." This way he gave blessings against himself and he accepted his defeat morally.

Yudhishthira also received the blessings of his teachers, Drona and Kripa, and of his uncle Shalya. He saluted everybody and went back to his camp. He asked his commander in chief Dhrishtadyumna to blow the conch. Then Bhishma also put his conch to his mouth. The sound of the two conches was the signal to all that the fighting had begun.

———◆———

❦

Bhishma Is Shot Down

For nine days Bhishma conducted the war as commander in chief of the Kaurava army. His father had given him a boon of dying at will. That meant that Bhishma could select the time of his death and the way in which he would die and that nobody could kill him if he did not want to be killed. It was one of his greatest powers. He was a great warrior and because he did not have to worry about wife and children or fear for his life he fought even more fiercely. It was terrible.

For nine days Bhishma demonstrated his skills in managing war affairs. The Pandavas realized they could not beat the Kauravas as long as Bhishma was fighting. On the evening of the ninth day, when the fighting had ceased for the night, they visited Bhishma in the Kaurava camp. They said, "Grandfather, without eliminating you we cannot win the war, so we might as well stop fighting and leave."

Bhishma was fed up with being commander in chief for Duryodhana. He realized he was only wasting his energy with a bunch of stupid people who were not going to follow dharma at all. It seemed the sooner the end came the better. He decided to quit and therefore he told the Pandavas he would not fight Shikandin who was the incarnation of princess Amba, his sworn enemy. Shikandin was a warrior in the Pandava camp who even had a son, but in the eyes of Bhishma, Shikandin was still a lady. Being a follower of dharma Bhishma would never shoot an arrow at a lady, so he would let Shikandin shoot at him without offering resistance.

The next day Arjuna took advantage of Bhishma's advice. Shikandin attacked Bhishma and from behind his back Arjuna also shot at Bhishma. Because the two men were shooting with different intensity and their bows had different power Bhishma felt how their arrows penetrated his body in different ways. So many arrows pierced his body that when he fell down on the ground his body was completely supported by the arrows. He remembered his ancestors and he saw the whole film of his life and the evolution of the war all at one time.

Bhishma was put out of action, but he was still alive. He remained lying on his bed of arrows. Every evening people would go and visit him. They paid their homage, told him who had died, and what had happened. Bhishma recognized everybody who came to visit him, and since he was related to everybody he was interested in their welfare. When Karna came and touched his feet saying, "Pranam pitamaha (greetings, Grandfather)," Bhishma said, "Come, son of Kunti, and stand near my head. From the first day I knew that you were a son of Kunti, but I didn't tell you before because you were so hostile toward Arjuna and I wanted to keep you away from the family." It was the first time that Bhishma treated Karna as a grandfather and consoled him.

Violating the Laws of War

Before the start of the war the parties had agreed to act according to several laws of war, representing a code of conduct on the battlefield. One of the laws stated that there would be no fighting between sunset and sunrise; at night people would visit each other's camps to see their relatives and to help the wounded. As long as Bhishma was commander in chief, the laws were respected and the war was fought in a right way. But that changed when Bhishma had been shot down. At sunset the conch was blown to signal that it was time to stop, but everybody ignored it and continued fighting. The laws of war were violated many times in many ways. The war had started with the aim of establishing the rule of dharma, but very quickly the spirit changed and dharma was forgotten completely. The aim of the war became obtaining victory—if not by right methods, then by wrong ones. This illustrates the basic human nature that at the beginning of a process we are idealists who want to serve truth and humanity, but during the process our selfish motives come up.

22

Corpses of Three Generations

Bhishma and Drona were followers of dharma. Both were bound to Duryodhana by their dharma—Bhishma because of his vow of loyalty to the throne and Drona because he was on the payroll of the throne. As he was paid by the state and living on that money, it was Drona's dharma to support Duryodhana even though Duryodhana was always rough with him, treating him badly, talking bad language to him, never trusting him, and always blaming him for being a well-wisher of Arjuna. It was true that Drona sympathized with Arjuna and under different circumstances he would have joined the side of the Pandavas.

Drona's Maze

On the eleventh day of the war Drona became commander in chief of the Kaurava army. The whole day Drona fought but to no avail. The next day Duryodhana was angry with Drona. He demanded more results. Duryodhana was the boss and everybody had to obey him. Drona promised he would perform better that day.

Drona wanted to arrest Yudhishthira and take him to Duryodhana as a

176

prisoner of war. But as long as Arjuna was around he could not do much because Arjuna was very clever and a good archer. He had been Drona's best student. They needed to lure him away from the battle. Two people offered their services to keep Arjuna busy on one side of the battlefield so Drona could capture Yudhishthira on the other side. But the plan failed because at the last moment Arjuna came back and saved his brother.

Drona tried to win the war by his skills, but people who do not work according to the law of nature lack merit and inner strength, which are also needed to succeed. On the thirteenth day Duryodhana was getting nervous. He told Drona, "The past two days we fought without any success. If you don't succeed today I will leave or I will commit suicide."

Drona needed to please him, but he could not make much progress as long as Arjuna was around. Another plan was made to divert Arjuna's attention and keep him busy. Duryodhana went to the Kirata tribe living nearby and said, "You only have to go and steal their horses. Even if you fail to take the horses they will come and chase you. Then you have to lead them away from the battlefield. That way we will win time to do what we want. You will receive ample rewards for your help."

As agreed, the tribal people attacked Arjuna's camp and Arjuna came chasing them in his chariot driven by Krishna to teach them a lesson. The Kirata men ran fast and lured Arjuna far away from the battlefield.

Drona knew how to arrange soldiers in a maze (vyuha) with the form of an eagle, a turtle, or a wheel (chakra), which was the most difficult of the three forms to pierce. The opponent was challenged to break the maze and it was considered a matter of honor to accept the challenge. If nobody entered then the opponent was considered defeated. The maze was very important.

In my book *Tools for Tantra* there is a picture of the wheel maze. It is called *chakra vyuha yantra,* but sometimes it is called *architectural yantra* because it was used as a design for buildings. That yantra is also used at the time of childbirth. Although nature helps by giving pains and the child is actively trying to come out, sometimes the mother holds the child in because she fears pain too much. Then this yantra is used to divert her attention from the pain and from holding the child. The mother is asked to meditate on the center of the yantra. Because her pupils are dilated she has to work hard to focus her eyes. If she manages to do so, the muscles around the womb relax and the child can come out.

In the Pandava camp the news came that Drona had constructed a chakra vyuha and that there would be a special war that day. Arjuna was the only warrior in the camp who knew how to enter the maze and get out of it again. Any other person who entered the maze would certainly get killed. Yudhishthira said, "None of us knows how to enter into the maze and getting out of it is even more difficult. Therefore we cannot fight and we have to accept our defeat."

He grew very sad and silent. Everybody in the Pandava camp was worried. Then Abhimanyu, son of Arjuna and Subhadra, though still a young man, came forward and said, "I do not know the whole thing, but I know how to enter the maze. If you allow me I will enter the maze and break it."

The other Pandavas were unparalleled fighters, but they did not know how to enter the maze, even the mighty Bhima didn't know. Yudhishthira asked, "This maze is very difficult and you never learned it from Drona nor from Arjuna. And Krishna, who taught you about martial arts, doesn't know it. So how do you know?"

Abhimanyu said, "When I was not yet born and had been in my mother's womb about eight months I had some consciousness. One day my mother was so restless that she could not sleep. She asked my father to tell her a story to divert her attention so that she could relax. Then my father told her about the chakra vyuha. He explained that it has seven gates just like the body has seven gates. Each gate is guarded by a powerful warrior. When you come to a gate you have to defeat the guardian before you can pass. After passing the seven gates you reach the center of the maze where you have to fight the king. Up to this point my mother had been listening closely, but before my father explained the way out she fell asleep, so the rest of the story I could not pick up."

People think that an unborn child in the mother's body does not know anything and does not register anything. They think that the child starts understanding only after birth. But Indian stories say that as long as the mother is awake and paying attention the baby is listening. When the mother sleeps it does not hear anything. Many people don't know about this and talk about all kinds of things with a pregnant lady. They should be more conscious that the subject they talk about may affect the unborn baby.

Yudhishthira said, "You are not complete in this art and not mature enough. You have recently married and your wife is pregnant. Therefore we cannot allow you to enter the battlefield."

Abhimanyu always had been considered a boy and he had not yet had the chance to show his courage and his skills in martial arts. He replied, "What is the use of a person who might save the entire family but who cannot do it because he has to care for his pregnant wife? If we don't go and fight today we will be declared defeated. But if I enter the maze I will be able to win some time because they can't kill me like that and maybe my father will come back and help me."

The four Pandava brothers thought that if Abhimanyu entered the maze and they were following him closely then they could slip in as well. They said, "If you enter then we will come directly after you and help you."

They agreed that the plan was worth trying, but it was wrong because Abhimanyu was inexperienced and he had never even seen a war. Similarly lots of inexperienced boys fought in Hitler's army. But it was an emergency situation and those who were there had to solve it.

⊙Y⊙

Abhimanyu Is Killed

Drona had heard that in the absence of Arjuna his son Abhimanyu was going to enter the maze. He went to Abhimanyu and said, "I am a teacher of your father, so I am like your grandfather. Please go back because this maze is too difficult for you. Your father is one of the few who knows how to break it. You will be trapped in it and get killed. You are recently married and I don't want to see your wife as a widow and I don't want your child to be born without a father. So please go back."

Abhimanyu replied, "A lion's cub may be small but still a lion. I am the son of Arjuna the great warrior and I am also a great warrior. I am not afraid of dying, so I will not go back."

Drona hesitated. He was a follower of dharma and it was against the laws of war for an expert like him to fight someone so inexperienced. He went to Duryodhana and said, "Today the war will be unfair and I don't want to be commander of it." But it was too late to step back. The maze had already been arranged and it was too late for Duryodhana to change the formation. Drona was frustrated because the day before he had not made any progress and he didn't want to enrage Duryodhana any further. Then he accepted the situation and said, "Whatever is happening is happening. I cannot help it."

Jayadratha had been posted at the first gate of the maze. He was the husband of Duryodhana's only sister, Duhsala. He hated the Pandavas and he had a boon that for one day he could defeat them all except Arjuna. When Abhimanyu came to the first gate followed by Arjuna's brothers Jayadratha only let Abhimanyu enter the maze and he stopped the others.

Abhimanyu was not properly prepared for entering the maze. Entering a trap without knowing how to get out of it is stupid, but he did it because he was overenthusiastic. Enthusiasm is okay, but too much enthusiasm is an enemy because it makes you stop thinking rationally and to attempt something without seeing the consequences. This story makes it clear that incomplete knowledge and being fascinated by something that you do not know can be dangerous. Similarly anybody can give you some chakra psychology for a couple of years, but they can't lead you anywhere. Sometimes students think they are mature enough to do everything and when they are not allowed to do something they may feel very restricted. But a student is an incomplete structure in need of scaffolding, which can be provided by those who know the game.

Abhimanyu had expected that at least Yudhishthira, who was a good swordsman, would follow him inside the maze, but now he was alone. For the first time in his life nobody like his father was around when help was needed. This was an opportunity to show what he had to offer. Although he only knew how to enter, he knew more than most people. He was eager to pass the other gates and reach the center of the maze. Each gate was guarded by a skilled warrior, but he managed to pass them. The fifth gate was guarded by Drona, himself, but he also got through. He passed the seventh gate and reached the center of the maze where Duryodhana was waiting for him.

Duryodhana said, "Good that you made it up to here, but you will not be able to go back."

Abhimanyu said, "Well, if I could reach here then I will also go back."

He was so strong that Duryodhana could not beat him. He thought his knowledge and power would enable him to escape from the maze, but that was impossible. The maze had been created by an expert, and a person with incomplete knowledge could not escape. The warriors who had guarded the gates joined the fight against Abhimanyu. Before Abhimanyu had been fighting one to one, but now he had to fight seven persons simultaneously. They demolished his chariot and cut off the protective armor that he was wearing. When all his arrows had been used and he had no more weapons left, he ran toward his chariot and took a wheel. With that he defended himself against the seven who were attacking him from all sides. He was overpowered.

When he fell down on the ground he said to Drona, "You taught my father the law of dharma and how to fight accordingly, but today you are not following the dharma yourself? I am alone, I have lost all my weapons, I am inexperienced and I am attacked by seven seasoned warriors. That is violating all the laws. You are fighting a dirty kind of war."

Drona said, "When I started the fight it was within my control, but then it got out of hand and I cannot stop these mad men."

Abhimanyu called them all by name and said, "All of you attacking at the same time is forbidden. Will you come and fight with me?"

But they ignored him and kept on attacking and they butchered him. It was a merciless death and such a brutal violation of laws that being burned alive would not have been enough punishment. As long as Bhishma was commander in chief nobody violated the law of war. But after Abhimanyu's death nobody followed it anymore. So in just three days the laws of war were abandoned completely.

Although Drona himself had not stabbed his sword into Abhimanyu's body he had been a party to the assassination. He had arranged the maze and as the commander in chief he was responsible. In conspiring against Abhimanyu he had done a hideous crime. When somebody who believes in law becomes a party to breaking the law he loses his inner strength. Drona lost himself completely. He sat down on the ground and said, "I wish I had died before this happened. But it is too late now. I don't know how to tell Arjuna how his son was killed." But there was no use lamenting. Drona took the dead body to the Pandavas to do the funeral rites.

———◆———

◉Ⴤ◉

Arjuna's Revenge

When the Pandavas saw the dead body of their nephew they were so sad that they did not know what to do. They wondered how they could possibly tell Arjuna when he returned from fighting the tribal people that the boy had been allowed to enter the maze without their help and how he had been killed. But at the time everybody had been thinking only about giving a reply to the enemy and showing they were able to do something even in absence of Arjuna.

That day the fighting stopped well before sunset because that one killing was so powerful that no warrior had enough spirit and strength left to continue fighting. The atmosphere around the battlefield had changed. In the Pandava camp the usual happiness had been replaced by sadness because with Abhimanyu they had lost their best educated, most dedicated, and most courageous young man. When Arjuna came back from fighting the Kiratas across the border he saw everybody sitting silent and sad. Nobody welcomed him. He felt something bad and asked what was the matter, but nobody told him anything. Then he saw Abhimanyu's wife wearing the white clothes of a widow instead of the clothes of a newly married woman. He could not bear it and asked her why she was dressed like that. Then she told him that Abhimanyu was no more.

Arjuna was sad to find out that Drona had been involved in the death of his son. He would have felt less bad if Drona had been a friend of Duryodhana, but he did not even like Duryodhana. He was an honest man who was not really interested in the war and who did not want to fight. Everybody except Drona was possessed by the desire for victory. Because nobody from the Pandava camp had been able to see who actually had killed Abhimanyu, the circumstances of his death were unclear.

Jayadratha was held responsible because he had guarded the first gate and prevented the four Pandava brothers from entering the maze to help Abhimanyu. Arjuna said that the man who caused his son to enter the battlefield alone should be punished. He took a vow that by sunset the next day either Jayadratha would have been punished or he would burn himself alive. Everybody believed the vow because Arjuna always was true to his words. In the Kaurava camp people were happy and celebrating because of Arjuna's vow. They only had to save one man for one day and then Arjuna would burn himself alive. They thought that by the next sunset the war would be over and they would be the winners.

Arjuna went to see the spot where his son had been killed. Standing on the battlefield, he heard a sound. It was grandfather Bhishma lying on his bed of arrows. He had heard the news and said, "Now the corpses of three generations will be burnt in front of my eyes. Do you know who did it?"

Arjuna said, "I think Jayadratha is responsible because he prevented my brothers from helping Abhimanyu."

Bhishma said, "No, not Jayadratha but Drona was responsible because Drona was the commander in chief and it was his job to see that his warriors respected the laws of war."

Arjuna replied, "I know my teacher. He follows dharma, but he eats the food of a selfish king and that must have affected his mind."

Bhishma said, "Everybody gets the reward of his actions and if your teacher has done something wrong he will get his karma back and he will be punished."

Arjuna felt guilty because when he shot Bhishma he was hiding himself behind Shikandin and that was against the law that said you had to confront and challenge your opponent face to face. If necessary a warrior had to warn his opponent to get ready for a fight. But Arjuna had tricked his grandfather.

Bhishma said, "Don't feel bad about that because you did it with my permission. Don't you remember that you asked me how I could be killed? I am the one who told you that in front of Shikandin I would throw down my weapons because he actually is not a man but a woman and I swore never to fight a woman. I am the one who gave you the permission and the opportunity to shoot me. Only if you had acted for personal benefit would you have broken the law. Don't feel bad; you haven't done adharma. By obeying me you have followed your dharma. But Drona did not follow his dharma because his desire to please Duryodhana made him ignore the voice of his conscience and the feeling that he was acting against dharma."

During the fourteenth day of the war Arjuna could not find Jayadratha. He had the right to challenge him for a fight and kill him but Duryodhana had decided to keep Jayadratha away from the battlefield for the whole day and let Arjuna search for him in vain. Then Arjuna would burn himself at sunset. At the end of the afternoon Arjuna still had not been able to take revenge. He was depressed and willing to die. He asked his brothers to help him to collect dry wood and make a pile of it.

But Krishna wanted to save him. To achieve that he played a trick, which was adharma. By meditation he produced clouds and darkness ten minutes before sunset. Nobody had a watch to look at and nobody questioned why the sun was setting earlier that day. So when it got dark everybody assumed that the sun had set. Arjuna laid down his bow and arrows, washed himself, and when the pyre was kindled he prepared himself to step into the fire. Krishna asked, "Why don't you take your bow and arrow in your hand and enter into the fire like a warrior?"

Arjuna said, "That is a good idea." He picked up his bow and arrow and concentrated on the fire.

Duryodhana wanted to see how Arjuna would burn himself. He was happy that in a few minutes the war would be over. He fetched his brother-in-law out of his hiding place so that he could also watch Arjuna dying. To while away the time they started teasing Arjuna saying, "You are a coward and now you are going to die as a coward. You could not even take revenge for your own son."

But then Krishna said, "No, look, the sun has not yet set." He clapped his hands and the clouds that he had created by the power of his meditation dissolved. The sun appeared and the illusion of darkness was gone. Krishna said to Arjuna, "You have your bow and arrows in your hand and the sun has not set, so you can still fulfill your vow. Shoot his head off, but let it land in the forest over there." Arjuna did so in a single shot.

Jayadratha was the only son of a saintly king. When he had been born his father studied the horoscope of his son and foresaw that some day his son's throat would be cut. The father made a curse that when the head of his son fell on the ground, the head of the person who had caused it would explode into a thousand pieces. Duryodhana knew this and he had thought that either Arjuna would be defeated and then burn himself or he would kill Jayadratha and then his head would be broken into a thousand pieces. Either way Duryodhana would get rid of his biggest enemy. But Krishna had instructed Arjuna to shoot in such a way that Jayadratha's head fell into the lap of his father who happened to be doing his sadhana in the forest. The father was horrified and threw the head of his son on the ground. The curse came true and the king's head broke into a thousand pieces.

———◆———

Apart from Abhimanyu, Arjuna had other sons fighting in the war. The story of Arjuna and Urvashi in heaven illustrates that Arjuna controlled his sensual nature and that he refused an invitation if it was not right. Still, he married girls from many countries. Except for Draupadi, he married only brides who were solely for him and whose motives were pure. You can understand this when you consider that Arjuna was the son of Indra and what Indra is in heaven fire is on Earth. Fire eats everything, so it combines with anything. Fire is also ego, which does not like to share everything but wants private property from a proper source.

By mistake Arjuna once entered the room where Draupadi and Yudhishthira were making love. According to the agreement between the brothers Arjuna had to go into exile. During that exile he met a lady and they married, but they met only once and then Arjuna left again. The lady was pregnant and when their son was born she used to tell him about his father, which inspired the boy. To see his father the young man joined the war and he got killed. By the end of the war all of the other sons of Arjuna would also be dead.

Drona Is Killed

It was the fifteenth day of the war. Drona appeared invincible and it became clear that the Pandava army could not win the war as long as Drona had a weapon in his hand. After getting rid of Bhishma the war had become a little easier, but now they had to get rid of Drona quickly, or the Pandava army would be destroyed after all. Krishna, Arjuna, Bhima, and the other warriors were brainstorming to find a way to kill Drona. Because he was extremely skilled in martial arts nobody could kill him in a face-to-face duel with arrow, spear, or any other weapon. Neither could they ask Drona how to defeat him like they had done with grandfather Bhishma. What could they do?

Everything is fair in love and war, so tricks are allowed. Drona had a weak spot. He had a son called Ashvatthama whom he loved very much, as every father loves his son.* Drona had no other children, so all his love was for Ashvatthama. Krishna said, "The only way to stop Drona is to dishearten him. If we can convince him that his beloved son Ashvatthama has been killed,

---

*I am not talking about those fathers who turn their son out of the garden of Eden or punish him in hell for a long time; I am talking about a real father who begets a son and loves him.

then surely he will stop fighting and it will be easy to kill him." But to convince Drona of his son's death would be difficult since Ashvatthama was invincible and could not be killed.

Krishna went to Yudhishthira and said, "When Drona hears his son is dead he will not believe it because he knows everybody is cheating. But you he trusts and if you confirm the news he will believe it." Everybody knew Yudhishthira never told a lie because he was the son of Dharma himself. He and his father both were called King of Dharma (Dharmaraja). If Yudhishthira said something everybody believed it. But Yudhishthira refused, saying, "I will not say anything that is not true."

Krishna replied, "Then we will make it true." There happened to be an elephant in the camp whose name was Ashvatthama. Krishna asked Bhima to go and kill that elephant. Many elephants were getting killed every day and it was nothing important. Krishna said, "Now that Ashvatthama the elephant has been killed will you confirm that Ashvatthama has been killed?" Yudhishthira said, "I cannot make a statement which is only half truth. I can only speak the full truth."

Krishna said, "Okay then just say Ashvatthama has been killed, man or elephant." Because Yudhishthira did not want to become dirty in his conscience he reluctantly gave in for the sake of war. Krishna told the soldiers in the Pandava army to spread the rumor that Ashvatthama had been killed. When Drona heard the terrible news he went to Yudhishthira and said, "Yudhishthira, I don't believe anybody; now you tell me what happened to Ashvatthama."

Yudhishthira said, "Ashvatthama has been killed, man or elephant," but as soon as he had spoken the words, "Ashvatthama has been killed," Krishna, Bhima, and Arjuna started blowing their conches and beating drums and they made so much noise that nobody heard the last part of the sentence. The trick worked. Yudhishthira was the only person who never had acted against the law of dharma. This was the only place where he deviated a little from it. Although he had spoken a necessary lie, still it created bad karma. Later he had to go to hell for a couple of minutes to pay back the debt he had created by speaking untruth.

Drona was devastated. He said, "Oh, if my son has been killed, then what is the use of my fighting." He threw his bow and arrows and sat down in the posture of meditation. At that time Dhrishtadyumna, the commander in chief of the Pandava army, came forward. He was the son of King Drupada and brother of Draupadi; both had been born to destroy Drona. He pierced Drona's body with a sword and on the fifteenth day of the war the teacher left his body. It was against the law of war to attack somebody without weapons, but nobody followed the law anymore.

The killing of Drona was a deterioration of ideology; it was one of the bad events in Mahabharata. In this moment it just makes me sad because I love Drona.

From the time of their childhood the hundred children of Dhritarashtra had outnumbered the five of Pandu. In addition the Kauravas had a big kingdom with many relations and friends who came to support them. At the start of the war the Kauravas army had 2,100 thousand soldiers, almost twice as much as the 1,300 thousand of the Pandava army. The army of the greedy people was bigger than the army of the truthful people because desires need more paraphernalia than truth. But naturally in a war between good and evil forces the evil forces are reduced more in number than the good forces. After fifteen days of war only a few of all the great people were still alive.

23

Kunti Loses Her First Son

Karna and Bhishma had never really been on good terms with each other. Bhishma and Drona used to put Karna down because of his humble birth and Karna always opposed Bhishma. Just before the start of the war Bhishma said such bad things to Karna that Karna swore not to fight as long as Bhishma was the commander in chief. He withdrew from the war. For ten days Karna just let things happen, which was a bad thing to do. When Bhishma had been shot Duryodhana asked Karna to become the new commander in chief. Karna was as skillful in martial arts as Bhishma and Arjuna. But Karna wisely refused, saying, "Because of my lineage many kings do not really honor me. You had better select somebody who is accepted by everybody." Then Drona became commander in chief.

But when Drona also had been shot there was nobody else left in the Kaurava army who was really suitable to be the commander in chief. On the sixteenth day of the war Duryodhana again asked Karna to become his commander in chief. Then Karna agreed because nobody else was suitable for the post and he wanted to defeat Arjuna and destroy Yudhishthira's kingdom. The charioteer who drove a warrior's chariot on the battlefield was very important because sometimes he saved the

189

life of the warrior. Therefore charioteers were selected with care and Karna chose Shalya, the king of Madra.

Karna Kills Ghatotkacha

Karna still had the Shakti astra given to him by Indra in return for his armor and earrings. It could be used only once and Karna was saving it to kill Arjuna. Krishna knew this and to protect Arjuna he asked Bhima to call his son Ghatotkacha. Ghatotkacha was Bhima's son by the demon lady Hidimba who came from a tribe that had mastered fighting with maya. The demons could create the illusion of fire or rain. They could become small as an ant but also so big that the whole battlefield would fit on their palm and then they would laugh. By illusions they could confuse the minds of the enemy soldiers completely and then finish them off. Because of these skills they had defeated all their human opponents.

Ghatotkacha was well versed in fighting with maya. He could stand in the air and put fire over the whole enemy army or throw big stones on it. He could create the illusion of night, the illusion of day, or an illusion of every- body becoming small. When he entered the battlefield he started throwing mountains on the Kaurava army. Arrows were shot at him, but they were like little pins that he broke and threw away. They threw a big net, which was like a small towel that he circulated and threw back at them. He became huge and floated in the sky over the Kaurava army, which terrified all the men and animals and made them feel they were going to die. Duryodhana cried out loud to Karna, "You are the commander of the army, but you are not able to save us."

Karna replied, "I can fight men but not a demon. What can I do?"

Duryodhana said, "Why don't you use that missile from Indra?"

Karna replied, "I am keeping that for Arjuna."

But Duryodhana was in such panic that he urged Karna to use the missile on Ghatotkacha, "If you don't use it now this demon will kill us all and there will be no occasion for you to fight with Arjuna. So either kill him now or we will lose the battle today."

Karna gave in and released the Shakti astra. It killed Ghatotkacha and returned to Indra, so Arjuna was spared.

———◆———

Karna Is Shot

Karna was an expert with bow, sword, and spear. At one point in the battle he defeated Bhima and he could have killed him, but he didn't because he had promised Kunti to spare Arjuna's brothers. In the fight with Arjuna he wanted to show his skills, but when he came face to face with Arjuna he forgot the mantra to release the divine Brahma astra weapon due to Parashurama's curse. He was vulnerable due to the lack of his protective breastplate and earrings that he had given to Indra and the missile that he had got in return had been spent. And then a wheel of his chariot got stuck in the mud due to the curse of the cow.

It seems unfair that Karna had so many curses and handicaps whereas Arjuna had so many assets. He had the great Krishna with him, he had the blessings and good wishes of his grandfather and his teachers, and he had Hanuman on his flag. But Karna was a demon who was destined to be killed by Arjuna and Krishna, so it had to be.

Karna jumped from the chariot to pull it out and shouted to Arjuna, "Wait, my chariot got stuck; let me fix this and then we will fight again. Remember the law of dharma."

Arjuna waited for Karna to pick up his arms and fight, but Krishna asked, "What are you waiting for?"

Arjuna said, "It is against the law to shoot somebody who is unarmed and if I shoot him now people will call me a coward."

Krishna said, "Remember that he was in the pack of seven who continued shooting at Abhimanyu although he was unarmed. And they killed him without any mercy. From the very beginning he has been wrong, but today this man talks about dharma. He himself has defied the law and he does not deserve fair treatment. There is no harm in punishing him. Shoot!"

Krishna had promised he would not lift a weapon or kill anybody in the battlefield, but nevertheless he said, "He is Sahasrabahu and we must finish him. If you don't shoot, I will." Arjuna was persuaded. He lifted his bow and put an end to Karna's life. The Kaurava army retreated when their commander in chief was shot down.

Rather than blaming Arjuna for the death of Karna, Vyasa puts the blame on Krishna knowing that Krishna is beyond all blame.

The Generosity of Karna

Karna was a very generous person. He would give anything within his means, especially to brahmins begging for alms. Illustrating this there is a folk story, which is not included in the Mahabharata.

Karna's Last Gift

Krishna said to Arjuna, "Today the earth loses the noblest character it has been bearing in a long time."

Arjuna thought he himself was the most civilized, the most gentle, and the most devoted person. He thought he was the only bhakta (lover of god) because he was Nara and a part of Narayana. He said, "I don't understand what you are talking about."

Krishna said, "Come, I will show you." He disguised himself and Arjuna as begging sadhus and together they went to Karna as he lay dying on the battlefield near his chariot. They could walk freely on the battlefield because the fighting had stopped. Standing near Karna Krishna said, "We are brahmins and we have come to ask your help."

Karna replied, "My whole life I have helped brahmins, so tell me your problem and I will try to help you."

The brahmin said, "We need a sheet, some cloth, and some fruits for the marriage of our daughter, but we have no money."

Karna said, "What can you beg now? I have nothing left; everything is finished."

The brahmin said, "The gold from your tooth would be helpful."

Karna agreed. He took a heavy arrow, hit his tooth out, took it in his hand and offered it to the brahmin saying, "Here is the tooth; the gold is in it, you can take it out."

The brahmin said, "It is impure because it comes from your mouth and we cannot touch it because we are brahmins."

Karna asked, "How can I purify it?"

The brahmin said, "You know the art of invoking deities. You can invoke Ganga and shoot an arrow in the ground to get water, wash the gold, and then give it." Karna recited the mantra of Ganga as he managed to pick up his bow and use his feet to shoot an arrow into the ground. Immediately a stream of water came rushing out. With that water Karna washed the tooth and then offered it to the brahmin saying, "Here is gold for you."

Then Krishna changed back to his original form and said, "I am not a beggar nor a brahmin. I am Krishna and he is Arjuna. I just wanted to show your younger brother the spirit that you have for charity and how you are devoted to dharma. Even when you are dying you don't say, 'Oh, I am dying and I can't do anything.' You still are willing to help somebody asking for charity. We think your name will remain in the history of the world forever for being very generous and we will miss you."

———◆———

Karna's Cremation

Karna said, "Krishna, you are the lord of the universe. Please give me a boon. I was born of a mother who was a virgin and I want my body to be cremated on a virgin piece of land where nobody has ever been burned or buried."

Through his yogic power Krishna went through the whole universe, but he could not find such a piece of land. For one time god felt sad that he could not really fulfill somebody's wish. He said, "I am sorry I cannot give you this boon because the whole earth is a graveyard. Everywhere on Earth bodies have been burnt or buried. If you want I can put your body in my hands and burn it. Nobody has ever died in these hands. They are pure."

Karna said, "No that is not needed. I just wanted to tell you that the body of this earth is so full of memories of death and suffering that no virgin place is left. Death comes for everybody. It is nothing wrong. I am only sad that my younger brother Arjuna violated the law of dharma by attacking me when I had no weapons in my hands and I was helpless."

Krishna replied, "As you sow, so you reap. You did that to his son and he did that to you. In future generations it will keep on happening. Everybody is somehow or the other doing something bad to everyone; there is nothing wrong about it."

When Karna's body was taken for cremation Kunti appeared. She never had accepted Karna, but now as a mother she could not resist. She saw Karna's dead body and fell down on it calling him her son. Most of her life she had been hiding that Karna was her son. Only a few days before she had informed Karna in private, but she never told it anybody else, so Yudhishthira and Arjuna still did not know. Yudhishthira said, "Mother, why are you here today? So many persons died. When Abhimanyu died you did not come to the battlefield. You are disgracing me by embracing my enemy who is from a low caste."

Kunti could not bear it. She said, "I have been silent all my life. I have never told it to anybody, but today I tell you that he is your older brother. If a bad word comes out of your mouth against this man then I will curse you. Many times I have heard people saying that Karna is just the son of a charioteer and he is bad and I did not say anything. But now you should not insult him anymore. Even when a bad man has died nobody speaks anything bad about him. How can you talk like this?"

Yudhishthira still did not understand and he asked Krishna what was the matter. Krishna explained, "Your mother is right. Apart from your mother only Bhishma and I knew that Karna was her son. Nobody else knew it. He was

born much before you were conceived, so actually he was your older brother."
Then Arjuna felt sad that he had shot his real brother.

Yudhishthira said, "If he was my brother I must perform the ritual, do the
cremation ceremony, and follow all the rituals of a brother."

Then Duryodhana stepped forward. He was full of emotion and crying.
He said, "Before you do anything I want to ask only one question. Arjuna, tell
me honestly, did you kill your brother or did you kill Karna who was a friend
of Duryodhana?"

Arjuna replied, "I killed Karna who was defending Duryodhana."

Duryodhana said, "Then you did not kill your brother." Arjuna agreed.
Duryodhana continued, "Then the dead body belongs to me because he was
my friend. I will do the ceremony for him. You have no right."

Yudhishthira said, "No, he is my brother by blood, the right belongs to me.
I will do the ceremony."

Kunti got up and said, "No, although he is your brother you cannot do
the ceremony. You never had any love for him. You never appreciated the
good in him. The whole kingdom appreciated him, but you five brothers
hated him all his life, so you have no right to do this ceremony. Duryodhana
has loved him all his life like a brother and a friend. He has the right to do it."
And so the dead body of Karna was given to Duryodhana. It was laid down
and cremated right near where Bhishma was lying, on the same spot where
the dead body of Abhimanyu had been cremated the day before.

———◆———

Karna's Character

The character of Karna is interesting and educative. He was partly
human, partly divine. He was a spiritually inclined person, honest and
extremely generous. He had a noble character. He was a man of principle
who believed in doing what he said. Most Kauravas were opportunists
but Karna was stable and solid. For Krishna he had great respect. He
was well trained in martial arts and a true warrior. He was ambitious in
the art of archery and considered Arjuna as his rival. A bad aspect of his
character was his resentment toward Arjuna. He was hostile to Arjuna

up to the end of his life. That originated in his previous life when he was Sahasrabahu.

Mahabharata shows that life is all the same and all different. The five Pandava brothers on one side and Karna on the other side were all sons of Kunti. Karna differed from the Pandava brothers because of his previous life as Sahasrabahu and because he was born before Kunti was married. She had not waited for a right time to invoke the divine power. As a result Karna was a premature materialization of divine energy. He was immature and suffered from an inferiority complex. His immaturity made him say bad words, deceive his teacher, and join the evil forces.

Karna's greatest weakness was not considering whether he had committed himself to a right or wrong person. Bhishma and Drona had the same weakness, but Karna suffered from it most. Because of bad company Karna became evil. Together with Shakuni and Ashvatthama, Karna was constantly setting up Duryodhana against the Pandavas. Duryodhana had given him status and a place in society. For that Karna was loyal to Duryodhana and ultimately even gave his life.

Kunti left Karna as a baby and he developed complexes and became an enemy of his own brothers. Similarly, there are many children growing up nowadays without knowing their father. These children suffer most because they don't get proper recognition. They can become enemies of their families, their country, and even their race. Forces destroying Western culture like the drug movement originate from people born as a byproduct of sensual enjoyment. Everybody has a natural right to live a healthy, happy, and inspired life. But if you deprive me of that, then I will have complexes; I will rebel and I will prevent a hundred persons from living healthy, happy, and inspired lives. That way I will demonically multiply my suffering.

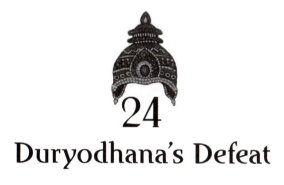

24

Duryodhana's Defeat

The last friend and protector of Duryodhana had gone. Duryodhana had trusted Karna more than anybody else and he had relied on Karna's archery to help him in this war. It drove him crazy. The huge armies had been decimated. Only five of his ninety-eight brothers were still alive. The only real warrior remaining in the Kaurava army was Duryodhana himself. He asked who would lead the remaining army. Shalya, the king of Madra, offered to do the job. He had been tricked by Duryodhana to join the Kaurava army, so he had not been fighting with his heart. But when Arjuna killed Karna when he was pulling the wheel of his chariot out of the mud, unarmed and defenseless, Shalya became filled with indignation. He felt that the Pandavas were getting crazy because of their victories and he should fight them. So on the seventeenth day of the war he became the commander in chief.

No Possible Compromise

Shakuni was still alive. He was a good swordsman and he attacked Nakula, but Nakula answered him well and knocked him down on the ground. Then he hit him with his mace, saying, "Look uncle, you did all these bad things and you destroyed the whole family, for what? In the end you are also on the ground. What did you gain out of all this? All your life you were jealous, you were bad, and you conspired, but what did you get out of it?"

That enraged Shalya because you were supposed to respect a warrior who had fallen down on the ground. He attacked Nakula. It became a fierce fight between uncle and nephew, which nobody had expected. Finally Nakula pierced Shalya's body with his spear and finished him without hesitation.

Duryodhana felt sad. All his brothers, all his friends, and all his sons were gone. Again he had lost his commander in chief and he needed to find a new one. He asked their teacher Kripa if he would be his next commander in chief. Kripa said, "Duryodhana, there is still time to make a compromise. Stop the war. I have been telling you this from the first day."

Duryodhana replied, "If people were still alive then it would have been okay, but now when all the great warriors have been killed and everything has been destroyed, it seems foolish to stop." All the soldiers in the Kaurava army supported Duryodhana, saying, "Although we know we will all die, we won't surrender. There is no compromise possible. Rather than giving up the fight we prefer giving our lives."

Then Kripa agreed to lead the army. He was the fifth commander in chief of the Kauravas whereas the Pandavas stayed under the commandership of Dhrishtadyumna from the first day till the last. After Bhishma had been shot, the war had been so fierce that at sunset torches were lit so that the fighting could continue. But a week later the fighting stopped at sunset again because there were not enough people left to continue.

Gandhari Curses Krishna

It was early morning around four on the eighteenth day of the war. Gandhari was sitting with her husband. They were talking about the death of their sons when Duryodhana, their only son who was still alive, came in to ask for her blessings. She asked, "What can I give you? I gave you all my advice, I told you in every way that you are doing wrong things, but you didn't listen to me."

He said, "To the Pandava brothers you said, 'Be victorious,' so you gave them a boon of victory, which you cannot revoke. Even a bad mother wishes good for her son; even if he is a robber the mother wishes him to be alright and live happily, but you blessed my enemies instead of me. That was wrong of you. You are not a good mother."

Gandhari replied, "I am a worshipper of Shiva, the one who does justice and justice only. My blessings are with my country and because you harm the country I cannot give you my blessings. My country is best taken care of by the sons of Pandu. But I still have something that I can give you. It is a power that will help you. Within an hour it will be sunrise. Go and bathe in the river and come back to me the same way as you were born, without wearing any clothes, not even a thread on your body, and I will make you invincible. Don't feel shy of me because I am your mother."

Duryodhana was interested in becoming invincible, so he went to take a bath in the river. Krishna was an early riser and he happened to see Duryodhana going toward the river nearby. He wondered why Duryodhana would go to the river early in the morning. He thought "He must be coming from Gandhari. Let me find out what is the matter." So Krishna went toward the tent of Gandhari. When he met Gandhari, he said, "Ram, Ram, Auntie, how are you?"*

She said, "What brings you here, Krishna? Pandu's sons are not responsible for the war and neither are my sons who are just stupid children. I cannot blame my husband for being greedy to be king. I cannot blame Bhishma for being loyal to the kingdom. Neither Drona, Drupada, Ashvatthama, or Kripa can be held responsible for the war. It is you, Krishna, who is responsible. You have the power to convince people, you could have prevented this war if you wanted and you could have stopped the enmity between Pandavas and Kauravas if you wanted. But you always play games and tricks and always create problems. You have been enjoying being the lord of three worlds for a long time and you can do everything, but you have never seen that a bhakta can have even more power. Because of you I have lost almost all my sons and the last one remaining has gone to take a bath and when he comes back I will

---

*Gandhari was an aunt of Krishna because her husband was a brother-in-law of Kunti who was an aunt of Krishna.

bless him, but to you I give a curse. One day your family of Yadhavas will meet the same fate. They will all fight among themselves and kill each other. As today I am grieving for my sons you will grieve for your sons and grandsons."

Krishna replied, "You have the right to blame me and curse me, but I can answer your accusations and tell you who really is responsible. When Duryodhana was born, Vidura told you that the child was born with bad omens: jackals were howling, owls were crying, and donkeys were making bad sounds. He advised you to get rid of the child because it would cause the destruction of Hastinapura. At that time your love for the child did not listen to Vidura and you let Duryodhana grow. I was not even born at that time; so this is rather your doing than mine.

"It was you who brought your brother Shakuni from Gandhara and let him live in the palace and spoil Duryodhana. Bhishma could not interfere in his affairs and nobody could because the king was blind and you were playing blind and we didn't want to disturb you. You covered your eyes because you were too loyal to your husband. And then you neglected your children and your duty. A mother who does not see what her children are doing is responsible for their problems. It is your fault and you are cursing me? Thank you very much. Because you are older than me and you are my aunt I should not say these things, but now what can you do?"

She said, "I can do a lot. I have power because I am a worshipper of Lord Shiva. Just as I have given you a curse and you will see that it will come true, I can also give a boon to my son and save him."

Krishna thought, "Oh god, she is going to give him some kind of boon that will support him." He said, "Your son must be coming back soon, so I better leave."

Gandhari Blesses Duryodhana

When Krishna left Gandhari's tent he saw Duryodhana coming back from the river. He was naked, not even a thread on his body. Krishna said, "Oh shame, shame, shame. You are naked."

Duryodhana replied, "So what? My mother ordered me to visit her like that."

Krishna said, "Yes, but you are not a child anymore so you should not go naked in front of your mother. At least cover your genitals. Even a leaf would do."

Duryodhana said, "I am confused, but if you say so I will do it." He went to a banana plant, broke off a big leaf, wrapped it around his hips and then went inside to see his mother.

Gandhari had had a cloth tied around her eyes ever since her marriage. When she noticed that Duryodhana had entered the tent she asked, "Did you take a bath?"

He said, "Yes."

"Did you chant your mantras properly?"

"Yes." "Did you think of anything bad along the way?"

He said, "I was only thinking about you."

"Did you meet any bad person along the way?"

"No, only Krishna and he is not a bad man."

Gandhari said, "Okay, then you are pure. Stand right in front of me. Now just for a minute I am going to open my eyes, which I have kept closed for thirty years. The light that will come out of them will be absorbed by your body and make it invincible. No sword and no spear will be able to pierce your body and no mace will be able to break it."

Saying that, she took off her blindfold and looked at Duryodhana who was standing in front of her. Rays of light came from her eyes and went through his body except the part that was covered by the leaf. She became upset and asked, "Why are you wearing this leaf?"

Duryodhana said, "Because Krishna told me so. He said that I should not go naked in front of my mother."

Gandhari said, "You listened to that idiot who always plays tricks and creates problems. Damned Krishna; this part will remain weak now. I have spent all my good karma to save you, but you did not save yourself. Now the tapasya of my whole life is gone and I cannot do the miracle again."

Duryodhana replied, "What does it matter? You have already blessed *the Pandavas and wished their victory, so I am not going to win anyway. Forget it."*

The Duel

After sunrise the war started again, but Duryodhana needed rest. His mind was completely out of control and he could not think anymore. He went to a pond near the battlefield and he sat on the bottom of the pond to relax. The people in the battlefield did not see Duryodhana anymore and they wondered where he might be. A villager who was passing by told them he had seen a warrior near the pond when he had taken his cows there to water them.

The Pandavas went to the pond and started sneering loudly, "Duryodhana, why are you hiding? Now there is no use hiding. Why did you start the war? If you were such a coward you should not have started the war."

Duryodhana could not resist and he came out from the pond. He said, "I was not running away. I am not a coward and I don't even love my life; it is useless now. I don't care. My shameful condition is more torturous to me than dying with honor. If I fight and die I am an honorable warrior and I have no problem. Why should I run away? But I was definitely tired, so I thought I would cool myself in this pond."

Yudhishthira said, "If you accept your defeat now we will spare you so that out of ninety-nine sons at least one remains to do the rituals, to offer homage to the father, and set fire to the dead bodies of his sons. If you like we can still compromise and the war will be finished."

Duryodhana said, "To the very last moment I will not accept my defeat. All of you are well armed and nicely dressed for fighting, but I am defenseless because I was just relaxing without my armor and my weapons. Out of you five brothers, whoever thinks he is powerful can fight with me. Or maybe you think you all should attack me together. Now I am not afraid of death and it might be even easier for me if you all attack me at the same time."

Yudhishthira said, "No, the last decisive fight will be according to the laws. If you win this fight then we all lose. You can select anyone you want to fight."

Duryodhana said, "All my life Bhima has been my biggest enemy, so I want to fight with him."

Duryodhana was given his mace and then the fight with Bhima started. If you hit a mountain hard enough, it will break, but when Bhima was hitting against Duryodhana's body nothing happened. While Bhima was hitting him Duryodhana was standing and not even moving his mace. He was laughing and waiting for Bhima to get exhausted so that he could then finish him in one blow. Krishna pointed at his hips to direct Bhima's attack to Duryodhana's weak spot. Bhima saw Krishna pointing and understood what it meant. So with his mace he hit Duryodhana's hip and broke his hipbone. Duryodhana fell on the ground. He was crippled and could not get up anymore, but he didn't give up. He said, "I am still not dead. Come and hit me."

Yudhishthira said, "No, once he has fallen down, you can't hit him anymore."

But Bhima was angry. He kicked Duryodhana and put his foot on Duryodhana's head saying, "Now this foot is your crown. For this crown you were fighting and did everything bad."

Duryodhana said, "Yes, when somebody is helpless then anybody can do this. You are such a strong guy. Even a child from the village can put his foot on my head because I am helpless. Now you only show that you are not civilized, no shame for me."

Yudhishthira really felt bad and said, "Bhima, he is your older cousin brother, you should not do that."

Bhima replied, "I really feel like tearing his body and drinking his blood. He has done so much wrong to me. He has always been conspiring against me. Even when I was a child he poisoned me. So now I really want to punish him."

But Krishna stopped him saying, "Bhima, you should tell Duryodhana that you are sorry and ask for his pardon," and Bhima said, "Okay, I will do that but not now. Let him suffer."

When the Pandavas started moving toward the battlefield, Duryodhana shouted, "You cowards, you cannot leave me like this, helplessly waiting for the vultures to come and eat me alive. Why don't you kill me? There is no use of leaving me like this. Kill me."

Yudhishthira replied, "We just punished you. Now it is your luck if you survive or if you die. If you survive we will give you shelter, and if you die we will do your last rituals. But we are not butchers, so we will not kill you."

Duryodhana cried, "Krishna, it was you who conspired to create this situation. My mother would have made me invincible, but you persuaded me to put a leaf around my hips. Because I listened to you my hips remained vulnerable. And it was you who told Bhima to attack my hips and because of that I am dying. It was all done by you. Nobody will hate me for what I have done, but everybody will know that Krishna was a trickster and hate you for that. I hate you and I hate the concept that you occupy in the kingdom.

"I had nothing and I am not losing anything. I don't repent what I have done. In war one side always gains and the other loses; this is nothing new. Warriors always know they may enjoy the fruits of victory but as easily they may be defeated. Nothing wrong with that, but you, Krishna, you are bad."

Krishna replied, "It is a game in this world that everybody blames others. Your mother blamed me and now you are blaming me, but see who is responsible. All the seeds were sown by you. Whatever happens to you is the result of your own karma. You have done bad things, so you got bad things. I have done nothing bad; I was trying to make peace, but you did not let me because you were greedy. Now you are dying for the kingdom and you cannot have it." Duryodhana was sad, but he did not repent. He embraced death with honor and he passed away from life.

Balarama, the elder brother of Krishna, had taught Duryodhana to fight with a mace. He had returned from a pilgrimage and he had been watching the fight between Bhima and Duryodhana. In fighting with the mace the warrior is allowed to hit the back and front of the upper body but prohibited from attacking the lower body. When Balarama saw Bhima hitting Duryodhana on his thigh he got angry. After Duryodhana had passed away Balarama approached Bhima and said, "Bhima, you have violated the laws for fighting with the mace. You have unnecessarily acted against dharma and killed my student Duryodhana. For that I will teach you a lesson."

Krishna knew Balarama's strength and he feared for Bhima's life. He said, "Elder brother, please wait a minute. Where were you when Duryodhana acted against dharma playing the game of dice? Where were you when Duryodhana acted against dharma asking Dushasana to drag Draupadi to the court and undress her? Where were you when seven great warriors including Duryodhana surrounded and killed Abhimanyu who was unarmed? So many times Duryodhana has acted against dharma, whereas Bhima has acted against dharma only once.

"When Draupadi had been dragged to the court Duryodhana told her to come and sit on his lap. Then Bhima made a vow that one day he would break Duryodhana's thigh. So today Bhima only fulfilled that vow. Warriors must fulfill their vows, but how could he do that without hitting the thigh? So please be just, elder brother, and think about these things before you proceed."

Although he was not convinced, Balarama was pacified and he did not attack Bhima.

———◆———

25

Picking Up the Pieces

The war was over. Vultures were gorging on the abundance of corpses lying all around. Few people were left alive. Some were searching for the bodies of their relatives. Almost the entire family of the Kauravas had been destroyed. King Dhritarashtra and his wife Gandhari had survived. Bhishma was lying on a bed of arrows, completely conscious, sometimes saying something but most of the time silent. Kripa, the last commander in chief of the Kaurava army, had survived. Still there was something bad that had to happen.

Ashvatthama had been declared dead to deceive Drona, but he was still alive. He felt that the Pandavas had killed his father by cheating. He threw the divine weapon of Brahma astra on the Pandava camp. At that time everybody was out except Uttara, the pregnant wife of Abhimanyu who had been killed in the chakra vyuha. The Brahma astra went toward her and would have killed the child inside her womb but Uttara invoked Krishna who took the Brahma astra on himself. Because he was Vishnu incarnated, the weapon could not harm him and it went back. This way Abhimanyu's son was saved.

❀

Ashvatthama Attacks the Pandavas

Ashvatthama was not satisfied. He and his nephew Kritavarma, son of Kripa, wanted revenge for Duryodhana's death. They waited in the bushes until everybody was sleeping and they entered Draupadi's tent where they found five men sleeping. They were the five sons from Draupadi and her five husbands: Prativindhya, son of Yudhishthira, Shrutakirti, son of Arjuna, Sutasoma, son of Bhima, Satanika, son of Nakula, and Shrutasena, son of Sahadeva. The sons were as courageous and talented as their fathers. The two assailants cut their throats, thinking that the men were the five Pandavas.

The loss of her five sons was too much for Draupadi to take, but Krishna said to her, "This would not have happened if you had been a little kind. You only wanted war and you constantly urged your husbands to fight. When I was going to make peace with the Kauravas you came to me and said, 'I have untied my hair because it was pulled by Dushasana and I will not tie it again as long as Dushasana is alive. If you go and make peace then how will Dushasana be killed and how will I tie my hair?' So when I went there I was not completely dedicated to making peace.

"That is how the war started. It was your game. For that I have been punished and cursed. For that Gandhari has been punished by losing her sons and Kunti has been punished by losing Karna. Everybody has suffered because you inspired your husbands to fight instead of feeling compassion. You did wrong by creating enmity between two groups of people."

But Draupadi again was adamant that the war had not ended and she said, "I will not take rest until Ashvatthama who has done this is killed."

When Bhima came out of his tent and saw the five beheaded bodies he got mad. His son Ghatotkacha had been killed by Karna; now Sutasoma, his only remaining son, had been killed by Ashvatthama. He got hold of Ashvatthama who was hiding in the bushes and brought him to Draupadi. He said, "Here is the culprit. What should I do with him?"

By that time Draupadi had been convinced that Ashvatthama should not be killed. Krishna had pacified her by explaining, "He is son of a brahmin *and son of teacher Drona. Killing him will bring bad karma. Your progeny will become crazy and nobody in the house will remain sane. You should not kill the son of the teacher; you should pardon him." So Draupadi wanted to spare his life, but Bhima was violent and furious and said, "I am going to kill him." Krishna stopped him from doing it and managed to pacify him as well.*

Eight people are supposed to physically stay alive for a thousand kalpas (days of Brahma). They cannot be killed and they are called "the eight immortals" (*ashtha chiranjivi*). They include Hanuman, Vasishta, Kripa, and Ashvatthama. Ashvatthama had been born with a gem on his third eye. As long as it was there nobody could defeat him, and even without the gem he would not die.

Krishna said, "If you take the gem from his forehead he will survive, but he will be as good as killed because all his power, intelligence, and wisdom are in it. So take it out."

Arjuna said, "I don't want to touch the gem, but it should come out." He took an arrow, chanted a mantra, and shot. The arrow hit the gem and Ashvatthama was left alive with only a wound on his forehead where the gem had been.

———◆———

Ashvatthama was left to roam around eternally. Even nowadays he is seen sometimes. Then people think that he is wounded, so they offer him water and things to clean his wounds. After being with people for some time he leaves again.

A New Beginning for Hastinapura

Krishna, Bhima, Yudhishthira, and Kripa, the family teacher and commander in chief of the Kaurava army, came together. The kingdom was given to Yudhishthira. People from nearby places were invited to come and restart the town of Hastinapura. Dhritarashtra lived for many years with the Pandavas in Hastinapura. In the end he left for the forest where he was consumed by tapasya. He and Gandhari left their bodies together.

Bhishma had a boon that he would die at the moment that he had chosen. When he had been shot it was winter, which was not an auspicious season to die since the point of sunrise was in the southeast. He remained lying on his bed of arrows near the battlefield where he had been fighting. From there he had seen many warriors dying in battle.

Yudhishthira among others used to visit him every evening and ask him questions about philosophy and religion. Bhishma actually was a celestial being who had been educated in heaven and all his life he had learned about truth, righteousness, and dharma, so he could explain questions of life, death, and karma very well. Lying on the arrows that were piercing his body, he would narrate dialogues between him and rishis on the subject of interest. Although he was in pain he did not say, "Oh god, what are you doing to me?" Instead he was enjoying life, telling stories, talking about dharma, and showing a high attitude toward life. Because he had followed dharma he had the advantage of remaining in peace, even though a thousand arrows of nonsense had pierced him and made him fall down.

Bhishma's philosophical discourses to Yudhishthira fill the final chapter of Mahabharata called Shanti Parva. It is about half of the total volume of Mahabharata, which shows how learned he was. He remained lying on his bed of arrows for several months until the springtime when the sunrise was in the northeast again, which was auspicious for dying. Finally he could leave his body and return to heaven where he once upon a time had been a Vasu, guardian of the northeast corner.

The Trials of Dharma

In the Mahabharata, Dharma is presented in three forms: Vidura and Bhishma as personifications of Dharma and Yudhishthira as the son of Dharma. Vidura was Dharma incarnate and he was the greatest advocate of dharma. He kept on telling the truth. When nobody was listening to him, he would withdraw because he was not a fighter. He did not take up arms but instead retired in samadhi. Saintly people are like turtles, who withdraw their head and feet into the safety of their shell when circumstances are not favorable and only come out again when circumstances have improved. Vidura was not a warrior; he was rather the son of a maidservant. For generations his family had only been serving the royal palace, so his genes told him to submit. Like that, true wisdom is humble, not aggressive. Among wise people, three quarters withdraw from the world like Vidura and only one quarter of them live inside the world. Some of them write books, give talks, make TV shows, and try to educate people, but they don't have much effect. The industries, which are the gods of today, do not allow wise people to present their statements. Wrong things are propagated more and more by TV, magazines, and newspapers. If you watch TV you get an advertisement for a product that is not environmentally friendly every five minutes.

Vidura's life is exemplary and I have seen a film on it. Also there is a book available in India, which is supposed to be written by him. It is called *Vidura Niti* (philosophy of Vidura).* It is a beautiful treatise on dharma and a code of conduct for human beings. It is full of good advice on living a simple, good, and honest life. It explains the valuable aspects of life. It tells how to maintain dharma and balance in life and how to face the evil outside.

Vidura was completely non-attached but Yudhishthira was a little attached because he was the son of Dharma: a good copy but not the original. He was bound by laws and he had some bad habits. One bad habit was gambling, which caused the entire drama.

Bhishma knew a lot about dharma because he actually was a Vasu from heaven born from Ganga, a very noble mother. After his education in heaven he was brought back to his earthly father as a gift of the god to the humans; that is why his real name was Devadatta (gift of god). Bhishma's story illustrates the trials and sufferings that a follower

---

Vidura Niti has been published in many versions by several publishers. You will find it in almost every third house in India, so it is quite popular. You can buy it in Sanskrit or translated into Hindi. English translation is also available in print and online.

of dharma has to undergo. His birth already was a punishment due to Vasishta's curse. Then he suffered because his mother took him to heaven when he was a baby and he did not see his father until he had become an adult. When she had left he suffered because he had no mother. He was the legal heir of the kingdom of Hastinapura and he took care of it. He had everything at his command and always lived in a palace, but he never became king and he never married. For a cause that he considered his dharma, he joined the side of evil and everybody called him bad. He was wearing white clothes, riding white horses, and bearing a white flag, but with all that white he was on the side of evil; that is Kali Yuga.

In Mahabharata more signs of Kali Yuga were visible as well, such as treachery, conspiracy, wrong politics, false promises, breaking vows. Things that make the energy flow downward became popular. Wisdom remained with some people, but nobody paid attention to what they said. Vidura was one of those poor people whom nobody listened to, but the poorest of all was Bhishma. He was a part of the divine consciousness that is not interested in anything but has to watch everything happening. He knew that the whole human community is one brotherhood and he wanted everybody to enjoy their own little share. But unfortunately he had to watch men being born, growing up, and treacherously swallowing the shares of others. And he had to watch them starting to fight for their petty desires, destroying each other, and the whole kingdom.

He felt that people had become rotten and did not care about anything anymore. This decay of dharma made him feel sad. He thought the world was going to be destroyed. It is true that the world is going to be destroyed because everything that has been created must be destroyed some day, but it is foolish to feel bad about it. It would be fantastic if it would end right now while we still are in good health and talking about good things, but it doesn't happen that way.

There are three obstacles (*granthis*) in the evolution of consciousness. They prevent energy (*prana*) from rising through the central channel in the spine (*sushumna nadi*). They are called *Brahma granthi* (attachment to the phenomenal world and sensual pleasures), *Vishnu granthi* (attachment to emotions, family, and friends), and *Rudra granthi* (attachment to spiritual powers). Bhishma overruled the Brahma granthi by sacrificing his kingdom and his sexuality so that his father could marry Satyavati. But he could not destroy the association of the throne of Hastinapura with his father (Vishnu granthi). His moral values guided him to sacrifice his whole life for the sake of the kingdom of Hastinapura and they gave him the power to stay determined. He was being fed by the Vishnu granthi; that's why he had to be pierced with all those arrows. Even then he did not leave his body; he remained lying on his bed of arrows every evening giving lectures about dharma.

Bhishma, Stranger on Earth

Many people think the hero of the Mahabharata is Arjuna. Devotees of Krishna say it is Krishna. People who are more just say it is Karna because he acted out his role so well. Some good people say it is Yudhishthira. And for mafia types the hero is Duryodhana because he controlled all people engaged in mafia activities. But the real hero of the Mahabharata is Bhishma. He had a long life; the story of Mahabharata starts with him and ends with him. The first few volumes of the Indian version of the Mahabharata consist of stories about Bhishma and dialogues with his teachers during his education in heaven.

From heaven where gods and rishis were living, Bhishma descended to a world of criminals. He always remained a stranger on Earth; he was born in a wrong time. His consciousness was not of Dvapara Yuga and that was fatal. He was a right person who knew much about dharma. He believed in truth and honesty. He did not deceive anybody nor did he have double policies. He was a man of determination. Once he had made a vow he never deviated from it. Because his vows were for the benefit of others he never felt guilty or bad about them.

Bhishma had lots of merits; his only demerit was that he made vows without thinking whether they were okay or not. He made several wrong vows because he belonged to a different age. It is a mistake we sometimes make and it creates problems. If you have not properly made up your mind about something then determination does not help. He made a vow of loyalty to the ruler of Hastinapura. That was a wrong step, like all right persons make wrong steps. Because of that vow he had to support the greedy Duryodhana and because he could not save Duryodhana he had to die. He should not have committed himself like that. If he had promised to support any king of Hastinapura who was right, then he would not have had to support Duryodhana and there would have been no war. When you promise to support something there should be an escape clause in case you find that you are supporting something wrong.

Another example of a wrong promise without escape was King Shantanu's promise to Ganga never to ask her anything. Maybe that was his most stupid decision, but without it there would have been no Mahabharata. The main thing in Mahabharata is that cultures grow up to a saturation point and then they have to slide down again. Time plays an important role because values are reevaluated and changed according to time and many values get destroyed. People who do not change according to time become like Bhishma.

He was a nice, learned, and gentle person. He was so well educated, so intelligent, so good, so big and strong, that anybody living near him felt like a pygmy and could not grow. As long as Bhishma was in the battlefield the new generation could not make any progress. This happens today as well. Every new generation feels that the old generation is an obstacle. To let the new generation survive the old values, traditions, customs, and morals have got to be taken out from the society. But it is for time to decide what is really valuable; that is a different matter.

The younger generation feels, "We are new, we know more, we have more chances, and we have more time to live, so we are really responsible. The old people are just sitting and wasting their life and time." When the older generation says something the younger generation protests, "You are old and you are talking of old times. What you are saying is outdated and has no more value. We understand things much better."

For six thousand years every new generation has thought they were very intelligent and they knew all the answers and then the next generation came and made them outdated like they did with their ancestors. Six thousand years ago people felt the same thing that they feel now. Somehow we have to stop this and start respecting each other. The Pandavas did not think that Bhishma was outdated or that he was not talking right. They respected old values and old morals and they were true to their word.

Causes of the Mahabharata War

- The demon Sahasrabahu (incarnated as Karna) had to be defeated by Nara and Narayana (incarnated as Arjuna and Krishna).
- Cultures grow up to a saturation point and if they cannot rise further, they have to go down again.
- The decay of moral values at the end of Dvapara Yuga enabled Duryodhana to find lots of support. Previously husband and wife had equal status, but in Dvapara Yuga society had become more male dominated and there was less respect for the female. Yudhishthira could gamble his wife in a dice game because a wife had become property.
- Bhishma gave his support to any king of Hastinapura, no matter good or bad. If Bhishma had supported Arjuna instead of Duryodhana, there would not have been war.
- If Kunti had not been so impatient to test the mantra that Rishi Durvasa had given her, there would not have been war. Abandoning her child gave Karna an inferiority complex, which made him hate Arjuna and support Duryodhana.
- Several factors prevented Dhritarashtra from becoming king: Satyavati's impatience to get grandchildren, Ambalika's fear of the radiance of Vyasa, Dhritarashtra being born blind, and Vyasa's and Bhishma's advice that Pandu should be made king.

Dhritarashtra developed an inferiority complex, which increased the enmity between Kauravas and Pandavas.

꧁ Bhima's power made him arrogant, which irritated Duryodhana.

꧁ Yudhishthira's weakness for gambling provided opportunities for Duryodhana.

꧁ Duryodhana's greed and jealousy helped to bring about war. The Kauravas always were dissatisfied and wanted more. They were so greedy that they did not want to give even a needlepoint of land to the Pandavas, and that created war.

꧁ The Mahabharata is full of revenge. Amba wanted revenge on Bhishma and she even reincarnated for that. Shakuni wanted to take revenge on Bhishma's entire family. Drona wanted revenge on Drupada and then Drupada did hard penance to invoke the birth of Dhrishtadyumna and Draupadi to serve as tools of destruction for Drona. Draupadi hurting Duryodhana was one of the causes of the war. Duryodhana wanted to take revenge on Draupadi and later Draupadi constantly incited her husbands to take revenge on Dushasana.

꧁ Shakuni hated the royal family of Hastinapura and created enmity between the Kauravas and the Pandavas. More than Bhima or Draupadi, Shakuni caused the war.

26
Arrival of Kali Yuga

After writing the Mahabharata, Vyasa felt sadness and pain in his heart because he had been writing about the suffering and destruction of great human beings. He had described how his own grandchildren who had grown up together became good and bad characters who could not exist together any longer so that war became imminent.

He asked Saint Narada for advice and Narada said, "Whenever you don't feel peace and you have problems, remember the life of Krishna and your sorrows will be gone. But only chanting Krishna's name is too boring and you will get tired soon; there should be some spice included. Write the story of Krishna's life so that when people read it their mind will get absorbed and forget everything else. That way knowledge (*gyana*) and renunciation (*vairagya*) remain in good shape."

Srimad Bhagavata Purana

Vyasa accepted the advice and started writing Srimad Bhagavata Purana, which is mainly the story of Krishna.* The story of Krishna is also a part

---

*Nowadays this book is popular because Prabhupad Bhaktivedanta, the founder of the Hare Krishna movement, made a version that is available in the Western world in all languages.

of the story of Mahabharata, but in Mahabharata Krishna is just a character who is almost the same age as his friend Arjuna. He may be the supreme godhead or consciousness, but there are many other characters who are also interesting. At the end of the Srimad Bhagavata Purana there is a speculation about how Kali Yuga will be and a part of it looks quite true. It starts with a story of Narada walking along a road.

∾❖∾

Chanting the Name of the Lord

As Narada was walking he saw a young woman sitting and crying near two old people who were lying unconscious on the ground. He asked, "Who are you young lady and who are these two men lying on the ground?"

The lady replied, "I am Bhakti (devotion, love of god) and these two are my sons. One is called Gyana (knowledge) and the other is called Vairagya (renunciation, nonattachment). With the coming of the Kali Yuga my two sons have become old and lifeless because in Kali Yuga there is no knowledge and no nonattachment. Real knowledge is disappearing and people are becoming attached and greedy."

Then Narada asked, "How is it that you look much younger than your sons?"

She said, "That is because there are always new people who love god and their devotion keeps me young."

Narada asked, "Can I bring your sons back to their senses?"

She said, "Yes, chant the name of the lord in their ears and then they will recover."

So Narada took his veena and started chanting the name of the lord, and Gyana and Vairagya opened their eyes and recovered.

——◆——

The Dark Age Begins

The two books, Mahabharata and Srimad Bhagavata Purana, are connected. One connection is in the story of Parikshit. When Abhimanyu was killed in Drona's maze his son Parikshit was still in his mother's womb. Boys without a father are not fortunate because they feel father-less; sometimes they say, "Father, why has thou forsaken me?" When he grew up Parikshit started ruling India. During his rule Krishna died and Kali Yuga came. Krishna was a bulb from which light had been brightly shining, and when the bulb was extinguished darkness came.

❧❦❧

Ignorance in Kali Yuga

When Kali Yuga arrived it went to King Parikshit and said, "Sir, I am Kali Yuga. As everybody needs a place to live please allot me a species of animal, tree, plant, or grain, or a type of metal to live in."

The king thought that if he gave a grain to Kali Yuga to live in then Kali Yuga would come in everybody who ate the grain. He considered giving a plant or a tree, but all plants and trees were helpful to humans and if people took the juice of the plant or the tree then Kali Yuga would come in them. He thought that he should not say the name of a grain, plant, tree, or animal because they all so useful for human life. But something that was not so useful in life was gold. It was not needed much. So he said, "Okay, Kali Yuga, from now onward you will live in gold." So Kali Yuga started living in gold and it became a keystone of society, the foundation of all currencies.

King Parikshit got absorbed in other affairs and forgot that he had told Kali Yuga to live in gold. One day he dressed with robes and ornaments to go on a tour and he put his golden crown on his head. During the tour he saw a rishi sitting in deep meditation with his eyes closed, but when Kali Yuga is on your head every saint looks like a fraud. The king thought that the rishi pretended to meditate only because he did not want to salute him. He decided to teach him a lesson. When he saw a dead snake he got down from his horse, picked up the snake with an arrow, and put it around the rishi's neck. The touch of the cold and dead body of the snake drew the energy of the rishi down. He opened his eyes and he saw the dead snake. He looked around and recognized the person who obviously had disturbed him.

He said, "King, you come from a noble family; your grandfather Arjuna was a great devotee of Krishna, and your father Abhimanyu was a student of Krishna. How do you dare do such a bad thing to me? I have been in this kingdom for a hundred thousand years doing tapasya here, but nobody ever treated me like this. Now I have to go and take a bath. Why did you put this dead body on my neck?"

The king said, "Don't you lecture me. I know you were not in samadhi. If you were in samadhi you would not talk to me. You just saw that I was coming and you did not want to salute me. I put the snake around your neck as a punishment for your trying to be smart."

The rishi said, "If you are right then let it be so. But if you acted wrongly by putting the snake around my neck then seven days from now the same snake will bite you and you will die."

The king said, "I have met so many people who talk like this. Nothing will happen." He went back to his palace.

But when he took off his crown he remembered who that rishi was and he realized he had made a big mistake. He said to himself, "How could I do that?" Then he remembered he had told Kali Yuga to live in gold and since he had been wearing his golden crown, Kali Yuga had been on his head. He called the royal priest and explained to him that he would survive for only seven more days.

The king said that he preferred to spend the last days of his life listening to holy scriptures. The priest went to Shukadeva Goswami, another son of Vyasa. Shukadeva had been a parrot in his last life and as a son of Vyasa he had been born enlightened. He had learned by heart the whole story of the life of Krishna written by his father. When the priest told him that the king wanted to hear the story he agreed to come to the palace. For seven days he recited it to King Parikshit.

All possible precautions were made to prevent any harm entering the room where the king was doing his sadhana. Everything was inspected and cleaned before it was allowed to enter the room. But on the seventh day the snake came to the palace, took the form of a tiny insect and sat down inside a flower that the king wanted to use in his puja. When the king took the flower *in his hand to offer it to god, the insect transformed into the snake that the king had put around the neck of the rishi. The snake bit the king and said, "Oh king, you thought I was dead when you put me around the neck of the rishi, but by his power I am alive and now you pay back your karma." Then the snake disappeared and King Parikshit died.*

———◆———

Mahabharata and the Game of Life

The Mahabharata describes events in the lunar dynasty of Bharata, the family of kings that ruled North India, starting with King Bharata and ending with King Parikshit. Many people think that it is about the Pandavas against the Kauravas. That story may be good for a publisher to publish and nice for people to read, but the Mahabharata deals with humankind in many ways and it can be understood at different levels.

Vyasa was a spiritual man with high pursuits in life who spent much time in meditation. When such an evolved person writes the story of his family he also tells the truth about human nature and human psychodrama. Each character represents an aspect of human nature such as attachment, confusion, lust, or greed. Some of the characters are easy to interpret in this way but others require some study. In any case, all aspects of human nature are presented by characters who take birth, grow, and have children. All principles of psychology are presented in their dialogues. The basic human experiences that appeal to everybody are depicted.

Many of the characters, problems, and dialogues of the Mahabharata show up in every generation, so we can recognize the characters in our own society. We may recognize them in our own circle of relatives and friends. Probably we all know somebody like Duryodhana who enjoys creating problems for other people just for fun. However, one problem is that any Shakuni may pretend to be a Krishna and promise enlightenment; then we start running after a fake Krishna thinking that we are improving our state of consciousness.

We can easily identify with the characters and feel their sadness, pain, and joy. This is called universality of appeal and it is an important concept in art. Authors like Shakespeare, Milton, Wordsworth, Shaw, and Goethe wrote stories about characters that are universal. Their insights are still quoted like proverbs every now and then because they are true for all times.

The war in the Mahabharata is between truth and untruth living in the same kingdom. On one side the main characters are truthfulness, honesty, determination, and selflessness, and on the other side are violence, aggression, crookedness, covertness, indiscipline, and lack of faith. Apart from being the story of humanity in general Mahabharata is also the story of each individual. It is an allegory about the human body and human consciousness. Vyasa wanted to show that the war that once upon a time happened in India also is the inner struggle inside each person. If we look inside we can recognize the good and bad characters. They are the good and bad sides of our own personality. Inside us are greed, jealousy, conceit, and attachment. But also inside us are truth, friendship, faithfulness, determination, pure ideas, and pure thoughts. The good aspects are always having problems with the other side of the personality, which does not believe in those high values. When I need something I should get it in a legal way, but sometimes I might accept getting it illegally by using power, stealing, or by threatening.

Basic Aspects of Human Consciousness

The real purpose of Mahabharata is to teach us the aspects of our consciousness that can be an aid or a drawback to our spiritual growth. To avoid becoming too psychological, too abstract and dry, Vyasa presented his teachings as the story of his family. People who are interested in spiritual sciences read it as a religious duty. The characters are most interesting because we can see ourselves in them. This makes Mahabharata one of the greatest epics of the world, which people keep on reading, generation after generation.

⚕ *Ganga* is the spirit of the Ganges River. Rather than being a literal river, she is lunar female maternal energy. In Haridwar lots of people say, "*Ganga ma*" (mother Ganga) or "*Ganga mata ki jay*" (victory to mother Ganga). They are not so stupid as to think that the river is their mother, but they say so because the river embodies maternal energy. All of the sudden changes, wars, fights, problems, deceits, intrigues, and tricks taking place in the lunar dynasty of Bharata were a female game. No such things happened in the life of Rama who was from the solar dynasty. His life is pure and simply a life of karma and karma yoga. That way the Ramayana differs a lot from the Mahabharata. When we consider the body as a battery, the two poles are formed by the solar and lunar contrast or the acid and alkaline balance. The two most important channels of energy in the body are the *Pingala nadi,* which is solar and associated with Yamuna, a major river of north India and the *Ida nadi,* which is lunar and associated with Ganga.

⚕ *Matsyagandha* (as Satyavati was called first) represents energy in primitive form and the fishy smell represents cosmic imbalance. At the start of the cosmic theater there is a lack of balance, otherwise nothing would change and there could be no creation.

⚕ *Vyasa* was born long before the war started and after the end of the war he decided to write down the story of his clan including himself. That is why he represents witness consciousness. Witness consciousness presents the essence of the experience of consciousness in an acceptable form. It puts all our impressions together and makes a story so that we can understand and learn from our experiences.

❧ *Bhishma* is the main character of Mahabharata. He represents sacrifice, determination, and the old values of the society. If you have given something without thinking about profit and loss, then Bhishma is important for you. Bhishma also is inside our body. Our genetic code is bound to save our body like Bhishma was bound to save the kingdom of Hastinapura. Our DNA molecules protect our body from lots of diseases and problems and they contain ancient wisdom. We are committed to old values and ancient ideas because of the DNA molecules inside us. Sacrifice is made possible by the information embedded in our genetic code, which tells us that sacrifice eliminates many problems and elevates our consciousness. This genetic information is very strong.

❧ *Vidura* is also one of the most important characters in the Mahabharata. He represents knowledge, intellect, justice, religion, and the saintly type of wisdom. If you are interested in pure law and justice, then he is important for you. All his qualities were connected with dharma. He defended truth and the common welfare. He was simple, honest, to the point, a lover of justice. His life was one of following dharma, doing his duty, and living a simple life with his wife and son. He and his wife were devoted to Krishna. Rather than living his own life he lived his life to serve others. He was a saintly person and a philosopher. Even Bhishma used to call him Mahatma (great soul, saint).

Vidura was a neutral observer who always said if things were right or wrong without any compromise and without favoring anybody. He always spoke the truth without caring about who might get hurt by it. He was devoted to the kingdom of Hastinapura and he was the prime minister of King Dhritarashtra. Although he served a king who was bad, he always said what was right. He often criticized Duryodhana and his brothers, which annoyed the king. Most of the time Duryodhana and Dhritarashtra ignored him or tried to shut him up. When we do something bad our intellect tells us, "What you are doing is not right." Just as Duryodhana disliked Vidura, our bad habits dislike the criticism coming from within. Most of the time we ignore the inner voice and we do what we want, but sometimes it is so powerful that we are compelled to listen.

❖ *The kingdom of Hastinapura* represents the physical body, which is attached to lots of things. Nowadays the whole world is like Hastinapura, ruled by blind ego.

❖ *Dhritarashtra,* the blind king, represents the blind ego. Ego belongs to the body; it cannot exist without the body like consciousness can. Normally ego recognizes what is right and what is wrong, but when it is guided by selfish motives it becomes blind. Dhritarashtra was blinded by attachment, ignorance, and greed but most of all by the desire for power. Desire for power created the problems. Dhritarashtra craved to be the king of Hastinapura.

❖ *Gandhari* represents devotion, blind faith, and the energy of Dhritarashtra. She blindly followed her blind husband. She believed in him; it would not have mattered who she married, she would have believed in that person. When she received the message that Dushasana had been killed she felt sad. She always was with truth, but as a mother she was attached to her children. This attachment has a great problem. It is a basic instinct (*vritti*). Yoga teaches us how to get beyond all attachment to avoid the internal war. But it is almost impossible to get beyond attachment. Even in yoga, once you have tasted the high state of samadhi, you get attached to it and you want it to remain in it. Nevertheless, one who loses all attachments can keep the highest state.

❖ *The hundred Kauravas* represent ego, the father of all desires, split into many, such as jealousy, hatred, cruelty, violence, and love of power. Of all desires jealousy is the most destructive. It creates lots of problems and it makes it impossible for people to live together; when somebody rises others try to put him down.

❖ *Duryodhana,* like his father, represents ego, but he also represents jealousy, arrogance, pride, and greed. He and his brothers were overambitious and wanted the whole kingdom.

❧ *Kunti* represents primordial nature. She is there to keep the energy of the world in balance. She is the force of integration, keeping everything together with divine help. This can be seen in her taking care of Nakula and Sahadeva after the death of Madri. If Kunti had been more patient and had not used the mantra before her marriage the war would not have come. But her impatience, her overenthusiasm, made her do it. Because of social fear she did not face the truth and then to hide her mistake she made more mistakes. Actions that we cannot tell others require efforts to keep them secret and they bring restlessness and problems. Kunti concealing the truth made Karna an enemy of his own brothers and ultimately it would even destroy her family.

❧ *Karna* represents jealousy. He was extremely jealous of Arjuna. Although jealousy is the most destructive of all desires, sometimes it can be constructive. For example being jealous about somebody's good qualities can stimulate you to become a better person.

❧ *Subhadra* was the younger sister of Krishna. She was loved by everybody, just as Krishna was loved by everybody (although many found him tricky). *Su* is "good" and *bhadra* is "lady," a lady whom you will love. Subhadra is love, dignity, instinct, and devotion.

❧ *Drona* represents loyalty and tolerance and his enemy *Drupada* represents intolerance.

❧ *Pandu* could accept everything, so he represents acceptance. When he had shot the rishi he took it to be his fault.

❧ *The Pandavas* are the five sons of truth. They represent the five elements and the five senses that connect the individual consciousness to the outside world.

 • *Yudhishthira* represents ether (*akasha*), associated with sound and hearing. On his chariot was the sign of an Indian drum (*mridangam*).

 • *Bhima* was the son of Maruta, so he represents air (*vayu*) and the sense of touch. He was humble, gentle, full of humor, and honest, especially if he was angry with somebody. But he also could be rude, arrogant, and disrespectful.

- *Arjuna* was the son of Indra and he represents fire (*agni*), which is associated with sight.
- *Nakula* represents water and the sense of taste.
- *Sahadeva* represents earth and the sense of smell.

❧ *Draupadi* represents the energy (*shakti*) needed to make the senses work and to put the sensory perceptions together. She also represents the energy needed for the individual consciousness to work through five elements or the five active chakras. She also represents the dormant kundalini energy.

❧ *The battlefield of Kurukshetra,* the most important holy place of India, represents the land of action (*karma bhumi*) where all the fruits of the actions are coming out.

❧ *Krishna* represents cosmic consciousness (supreme consciousness, truth) that guides our internal war with attachments and teaches us how to fight. He helps the five elements to live in a right way. Krishna as a neutral observer saw Arjuna as a preserver of humanity and Duryodhana as a destroyer of humanity. Duryodhana was arrogant, unjust, dishonest, and trying to destroy peace and harmony of the people. Therefore Krishna was on the side of Arjuna. It means consciousness is with the preserver.

❧ *Arjuna* represents the individual consciousness, which likes or dislikes things. Arjuna fights the forces that direct the energy in a wrong direction and Krishna helps him. When Arjuna was bound by attachments he needed Krishna to remove his delusion. Arjuna is a symbol of human being with all the problems and weaknesses of an ordinary human being.

The Game of Life

To understand all the characters in the Mahabharata you have to understand life itself. But the game of life is so difficult that it cannot be easily explained. Each time you start understanding the game of life something happens that makes you feel you misunderstood it. We can see this in the stories of Narada. He was a wise man. Many times he thought he had realized everything and maya could not touch him anymore, but then he was caught by it again. The game of maya is the highest problem in understanding everything. Rishis have tried to explain maya with a small network of concepts that everyone can understand.

Static and Dynamic Aspects of Energy

The whole game of the cosmos is played by energy. Energy has no gender, but it does have a static and a dynamic aspect, which are often personified as male and female. The static aspect is the reservoir of the dynamic part, similar to the point from which the big bang started and out of which came nebulous material, galaxies, solar systems, and everything else. The static aspect is called Shiva or *purusha*. It never changes; nothing can reduce it or increase it. The static and dynamic aspects of energy balance each other. What we call *energy* actually is the dynamic aspect of energy. According to Buddhism it is male, but according to all other ways of understanding it is female. In Indian philosophy there are many names for the dynamic aspect of energy. When it has the power of obscuring vision it is called *maya* and when it becomes friendly through your own self-realization it is called Shakti, *prakriti, leela,* or *adhya.*

Three Forms of Energy

Energy works in three forms or phases: *sattva* (essence), *rajas* (action), and *tamas* (inertia). These three phases create a movement in energy. Rajas converts tamas into sattva and back again into tamas. This results in an evolution of *ahamkara* (ego identification) because something is happening inside. The phase of the ahamkara governs the nature of the things it creates: sattvic, rajasic, or tamasic. Sattvic ahamkara produces sense organs, intellect, and mind. Rajasic ahamkara creates work organs. And tamasic ahamkara creates smell, taste, color, touch, and sound, which are called *tanmatras* (rudimentary elements); then it creates the elements akasha (space), air, fire, water, and earth. So, the five elements are created by tamasic ahamkara; activity inside them is expressed through the work organs; and the intelligence inside them is perceived through the sense organs. Their activity is the light and their intelligence is the wisdom behind the light. The five elements create and preserve life.

As energy has three forms, a human being has three sides. When the sattvic side dominates, then spiritual and divine energy prevails. When the rajasic side dominates, a person becomes very active. In tamasic form, the person either becomes obsessed by fear, anxiety, and anger, and rebels against human values, or becomes dull, passive, inactive, and acts like a robot or a slave. In a person without personal desires only the desire for survival remains. A person who is struggling to survive will seek somebody's protection and help. Such a person may join a particular army, fight for a hero, take other person's lives, and even give his own life. Actually he has no bad feelings toward the ones he fights; he only fights for his survival. This is the life of a slave. This is the tamasic side of being human.

The Play of the Elements

Our bodies are made of elements and what we eat is made of elements, so elements eat elements. If there were no taste inside your tongue then even the best food would have no taste. Sometimes in extreme cold the smell and taste senses are gone and then nothing tastes good. Also in sickness, no matter how well the food is cooked, it doesn't taste good. So taste is inside you. Similarly touch, smell, sound, and color are inside you. Taste is enjoying taste, touch is enjoying touch, smell is enjoying smell, sound is enjoying sound, and sight is enjoying sight. When some element dominates in your mind a particular feeling comes that guides your behavior and your thoughts. Everything that you think, feel, see, hear, touch, smell, and taste is the elements. So we are all puppets in the hands of elements. The five elements are the main characters of the theater of life. This is also explained in my books, *Breath, Mind, and Consciousness* (Rochester, Vt.: Destiny Books, 1989), *Chakras,* and *Leela.*

In the body the elements work through chakras. Chakras are the seats of the elements from where we view the theatre of life. When our eyes are in a particular chakra the whole world seems to be filled with that chakra; when our eyes are away from that chakra the vision goes away. The elements earth and water cause attachment. Fire and air cause a little detachment and akasha total detachment. Attachment and detachment, outside and inside, expression and impression are pulsating: they increase and then they decrease. So elements are playing with elements and all the time we take this illusion to be reality.

Elements Need Consciousness

One of many ways of seeing the war of Mahabharata is as the natural war between the elements and desires of the body. This war is going on within us all the time. The five elements are the actors in the game of life. Their cousins who belong to the same kingdom are the desires. Because of ego there is a war going on inside us: desires continuously create problems for the elements. Desires waste our energy and cause conflicts and problems. When desires make us act wrong, our energy suffers; for example when you eat a meal in the middle of the night and then go to bed, the food is not digested properly and the energy gets disturbed. Wrong actions, working against the laws of nature, indiscipline, and especially violence attack the energy inside the body and that way cause problems for the elements.

In the war between the elements and the desires Krishna helps the elements. The elements are the body and Krishna is consciousness. Krishna is the charioteer who takes Arjuna on his chariot through the war in Mahabharata. Arjuna is the one who identifies with "me" and "mine" in the battlefield of life. You could call it ego, but this ego is necessary for survival. I would rather call it individual consciousness. Arjuna and Krishna are individual and supreme consciousness. The five elements belong to primordial nature (prakriti), but you are consciousness (purusha). You are not enjoying anything yourself because you are not the five elements; you are the consciousness that empowers the elements. As long as the elements are connected with the consciousness they are men, women, vegetables, fruits, sweet dish, everything. But when the consciousness (the living principle) is gone, what is left is a dead body that cannot do anything. The elements need consciousness to be alive. The elements cannot enjoy themselves if consciousness is not there.

The five elements have one wife, which is the kundalini that lives in the earth element and moves through water, fire, air, and akasha into a place where none of the five exist; then it joins with its true counterpart, which is supreme consciousness.

Essence of Indian Culture

Several stories in Mahabharata show a consciousness that is not bound by past, present, and future. Indian philosophy does not consider birth and death as the beginning and end of life. Rather it is believed that a person goes through a series of lives, as can be seen in the stories of Karna, Bhishma, Vidura, and others. It is believed that events without apparent cause in this life are rooted in a past life and if you could know the story of that life then you would better understand the present. Although it is difficult to find out about your past life there are methods because persons who can see into the future can also see into the past. You can go to places in India where the *Brighu Samhita* scripture is kept. If you give your place, date, and time of birth they will bring you a piece of paper from the old script describing what kind of person you were in your last life, how you lived, and what happened.

In all stories and classical epics of the world good and evil are clearly divided in two camps like on a chess board. But in Mahabharata there are good and bad people in both camps. Bhishma, Drona, Karna, Ashvatthama, and Kripa are ideal people who are on the same side as the evil Duryodhana, Dushasana, and Shakuni. Good and bad overlap. Similarly, following dharma can imply violating it. On several occasions Krishna himself manipulates the truth. When Arjuna was about to throw himself on the pyre Krishna created the illusion of darkness to lure Jayadratha out of his hiding place. And Krishna deceived Drona by convincing him that his son Ashvatthama had been killed. In both situations Krishna compromised the truth.

Mahabharata contains lessons on yoga and the highest lesson is in the Bhagavad Gita with the teachings of Krishna to Arjuna. All great prophets deliver a message from their father in heaven, but Krishna says, "I am the father and I tell you that to find your real self you should not identify with your alluring senses, nor with your instincts, nor with your genetic code." Mahabharata is the essence of experience of Indian culture. It describes how to achieve a better place in life and how to finally leave this body and merge into cosmic consciousness.

Index

233

About Harish Johari

Harish Johari was born on May 12, 1934, in Faridpur, a small village in Uttar Pradesh, India. In 1937 his family moved to their ancestral home in Bareilly. From childhood Harish Johari was gifted with sharp intelligence, amazing memory, and multiple artistic talents. A considerable portion of his wide knowledge and talent came from his family background. His father, Bankey Behari Lal Johari, was a magistrate, a practitioner of Vedic astrology and hatha yoga, and a student of Vedanta. Both of Harish's parents served as role models for him, as did his grand uncle, Acharya Chandrashekar Shastri, who had a great command of many subjects and wrote more than one hundred books.

Because his father's career as a magistrate caused frequent moves for the family, Harish was educated in many different cities. He received his B.A. in philosophy in Jaunpur in 1953. Also in Jaunpur he joined the wrestling ground, where famous wrestlers of his country instructed him in wrestling, body culture, and massage. When the family lived in Rampur, Harish joined a circle of poets and musicians where he met Jagdish Mohan, a well-known singer and composer, who became his lifelong friend. Music was another field in which Harish combined his creativity and his power of analysis. He studied the effects of sound on consciousness and the nervous system, composed and recorded a large body of meditative musical compositions, and was invited to lecture on music in the West.

In 1957 Harish completed his M.A. in philosophy at the college in Bareilly. In 1959 he obtained a second master's degree in Urdu at the university in Lucknow. His skills in Urdu poetry brought him into the company of Sufi saints, and he gained a reputation at poets' gatherings and competitions.

After his wedding in 1962, he made sculpting his profession, having worked with clay sculptures from childhood onward. The first order Harish got was for a huge sculpture of the monkey god Hanuman for a temple in Bareilly. While sculpting in the temples, he came in close contact with the saints who lived there. He questioned them about a wide range of subjects connected to the sculptures he was making and began to see that everything in the universe is interwoven. Through his work at the Hindu temples Harish developed his own unified view of matter, spirit, and mind. But most of all his work in the temples made him a noble *bhakta,* a lover and worshipper of God.

Simultaneously he developed his painting skills. It was a family tradition to paint the life story of Lord Krishna on a wall as a fresco, every year on Krishna's birthday. Yet Harish's special style of wash painting evolved with the help and guidance of his art teacher, Master Chandra Bal, in Bareilly.

In 1967 Harish met Dr. Richard Alpert, who later became known as Baba Ram Dass, and soon Harish was invited to visit the United States. Once in America, Harish was introduced to artists, scientists, and scholars who were interested in the ancient wisdom of Hindu philosophy and Indian culture. He explained to them the principles of ayurveda, swara yoga, Tantra, chakras, and mantras as well as many other sciences. In 1974 his first book, *Dhanwantari,* was published in America. From 1976 onward, Harish regularly visited America and Europe, where he lectured on many subjects such as painting, Indian psychology, dreams, and numerology. In 1983 Harish met Ehud Sperling in New York, and Ehud soon became a close friend and confidant and Inner Traditions the publisher of all Harish's books and musical recordings.

Harish Johari left his body on August 20, 1999, at his home in the holy town of Hardwar. He was a complete human being who enjoyed life as divine *leela,* a play of cosmic consciousness. He lectured and taught the art of living in awareness, knowing that all knowledge lives only when it is shared with others.

Also by Harish Johari

Attunements for Dawn and Dusk
Music to Enhance Morning and Evening Meditation

Attunements for Day and Night
Chants to the Sun and Moon

Ayurvedic Healing Cuisine

Ayurvedic Massage
Traditional Indian Techniques for Balancing Body and Mind

Breath, Mind, and Consciousness

Chakras
Energy Centers of Transformation

Dhanwantari
A Complete Guide to the Ayurvedic Life

The Healing Power of Gemstones
In Tantra, Ayurveda, and Astrology

The Monkeys and the Mango Tree
Teaching Stories of the Saints and Sadhus of India

Numerology
With Tantra, Ayurveda, and Astrology

The Planet Meditation Kit
How to Harness the Energy of the Planets for
Good Fortune, Health, and Well-Being

Sounds of Tantra
Mantra Meditation Techniques from *Tools for Tantra*

Sounds of the Chakras

Tools for Tantra

The Yoga of Snakes and Arrows
The Leela of Self-Knowledge

INNER TRADITIONS • BEAR & COMPANY
P.O. Box 388
Rochester, VT 05767
1-800-246-8648
www.InnerTraditions.com